TRAPPED IN TERROR BAY

Solving the Mystery of the Lost Franklin Expedition

Sigmund Brouwer

Kids Can Press

CONTENTS

Previous page: *HMS* Erebus *and* Terror *in the Antarctic,* by John Wilson Carmichael

Officers of the Franklin expedition (left to right): Captain Sir John Franklin (commanding officer),
Captain Crozier (HMS *Terror*), Commander Fitzjames (HMS *Erebus*), Lieutenant Gore, Stephen Stanley (surgeon),
Lieutenant LeVesconte, Lieutenant Couch, Lieutenant Fairholme, C. Osmer (purser), Lieutenant DesVoeux,
Lieutenant Sargent, J. Reid (ice master), H. Goodsir (assistant surgeon), H. F. Collins (second master)

AUTHOR'S NOTE

Perhaps the best modern comparison to Sir John Franklin's polar expedition of 1845 is the Apollo 11 voyage to the moon and back in 1969.

Both were outfitted with the most advanced technology of their time. Both captured public imagination across the world. Both had high expectations of success. Both were an incredible reach of human exploration.

The ending of each adventure, as we already know, was the biggest difference. Apollo 11 succeeded on an epic level. Franklin's ships — HMS *Erebus* and HMS *Terror* — disappeared with all officers and crew, the expedition becoming an epic failure and a mystery that remained unsolved for decades.

Today, it's easier to understand how Franklin's voyage faced almost certain doom even before the ships set sail. First, the obstacles were badly underestimated. We now know that there are a half dozen or so ways to snake through the Arctic islands and find passage from the Atlantic Ocean to the Pacific Ocean. Franklin, however, headed into uncharted waters, where ice made it near impossible to find those passages, let alone travel them.

It is such a difficult accomplishment that, although the Northwest Passage was crossed by ship and sledges in one of the early searches for Franklin, nobody successfully

HMS Erebus *in the Ice, 1846*, by François Etienne Musin

navigated it entirely by ship until almost a half century later, in 1906. Nor was that first Arctic ship crossing accomplished in a single season. After that, it took another 34 years before it was traversed again, another voyage that took two years.

The first successful commercial passage from the Atlantic to the Pacific through the Arctic required an oil tanker with a protective steel sheath fully 3 m (10 ft.) thick. The ship's navigators used computers and satellite photographs and sent helicopters ahead to survey and keep them updated on changing ice conditions. The ship was also accompanied by two icebreakers. Even so, the oil tanker was trapped by ice and suffered such damage it had to be docked for months for repairs. This was in 1969, almost 125 years after the *Terror* and *Erebus* set sail, and the same year the Apollo 11 crew landed on the moon.

Part of the incredible drama of the story of the Franklin expedition comes from understanding how crucial decisions made differently along the way could have saved the ships. Yet, as forensic techniques reveal today, the expedition's failure was as much a medical disaster as it was a vast underestimation of the journey's perils. During the voyage into the harshest winters on record, officers and crew began to die for what seemed inexplicable reasons. Reports of the desperate measures they took to try to survive seemed unbelievable at the time.

This is the journey that I hope you'll take with me in the pages of this book.

You'll begin each episode in command of the HMS *Terror*, as the man who earned the name Aglukkaq during his first winters in the Arctic.

In the second part of each episode, you'll see the mystery through the eyes of those left behind in England, as they searched first for reasons to celebrate and then for clues to the fate of the vanished expedition. You'll also find out about some of the changes and innovations taking place back home at the same time as the journey.

Each episode concludes with a detective story that combines modern forensic techniques with clues from Inuit stories passed from one generation to the next, and finally reveals the fates of the ships and men. Over the years, historians have proposed different theories, but these have evolved as science has advanced and the accuracy of Inuit traditional knowledge has been acknowledged.

Throughout, you will see how the techniques of forensic science help historians, geographers, archaeologists and scientists in the same way they help detectives examine a crime scene and courts of law apply scientific knowledge to legal problems.

In the end, though, you will have to weigh the evidence and decide for yourself: What truly happened in the final tragic days of the HMS *Erebus* and HMS *Terror*?

— Sigmund Brouwer

EPISODE ONE

Heroes Depart

TIMELINE

MAY 1845: THE DOCKS AT GREENHITHE, THAMES RIVER, LONDON, ENGLAND

JULY 1845: DISKO BAY, GREENLAND

AUGUST TO SEPTEMBER 1845: LANCASTER SOUND

SEPTEMBER 1845 TO AUGUST 1846: BEECHEY ISLAND

AUGUST TO SEPTEMBER 1846: PEEL SOUND AND FRANKLIN STRAIT

SEPTEMBER 1846: KING WILLIAM ISLAND

SEPTEMBER 1846 TO JUNE 1847: LAT 70°05' N, LONG 98°23' W

JUNE 1847 TO APRIL 1848: SHIPS LOCKED IN ICE

AUGUST 1848: BOOTH POINT, KING WILLIAM ISLAND

SEPTEMBER 1848: MONTREAL ISLAND, MOUTH OF THE BACK RIVER

HUDSON BAY

NORTH AMERICA

PACIFIC OCEAN

CANADA

UNITED STATES

GREENLAND

ICELAND

NORTH SEA

London,
England

EUROPE

NORTH
ATLANTIC
OCEAN

YOUR EXPEDITION : Aglukkaq

May 1845: The docks at Greenhithe, Thames River, London, England

GREAT BRITAIN

London

Greenhithe

"We have got 10 000 cases of preserved ready cooked meats on board the Erebus *alone so you see there is no chance of starving."*

— Assistant surgeon Harry Goodsir, serving on the HMS *Erebus*

Captain Francis Crozier's portrait, taken just before the expedition

This should be your greatest moment of pride. You are about to embark on the voyage that will bring glory and riches to England. But your heart is too broken, your sense of dread too great and your premonitions of doom too heavy.

It is late spring. The sky is cloudy and you are standing at a place of honor on the deck of a ship named *Terror*.

On the docks below you is a full band playing patriotic music. You can barely hear it above the noise of a mob of 10 000 gathered to cheer and wave at the departure of your ship and its companion, Her Majesty's Ship (HMS) *Erebus*. For weeks, the newspapers have been full of accounts of the preparations for this journey, and how England would claim the glory of becoming the first to conquer the Arctic in a quest to find the shortest passage from the Atlantic to the Pacific. To the public, you are seen as heroes. The reality is that you simply have a job to do.

Finally, tugboats are ready to pull the *Terror* and *Erebus* from the docks into the Thames River, then downstream from London, where once they reach the North Sea, the sails will be set for a voyage through the Arctic — a journey destined to assure lifelong fame for the commanders of the expedition.

You are wearing gold-striped royal blue trousers and a double-breasted suit coat with 16 gold buttons and gold-fringed stripes on your shoulders. The uniform shows at a glance that you are a captain in the world's most powerful navy. Indeed, because of the newspaper accounts, all of England recognizes you as second-in-command of the most technologically advanced expedition in history.

You began your career at age 13 as a first-class volunteer — looked down upon because you are "coarse Irish" among the English gentlemen whose family connections gave them every advantage you were denied, even though your father was a lawyer. Thanks to 35 years of service on every type of ship in every type of water, you taught yourself all you needed to know to pass examination after examination and rise in the ranks of the Royal Navy.

Few men have your knowledge and experience with ships in the icy waters of the most northern and southern reaches of the globe.

It was under your command on this very same ship, the *Terror* — with your friend James Clark Ross as commander of the *Erebus* — that you completed a four-year expedition to the Antarctic, narrowly escaping death there. Some have acknowledged that trip as one of the greatest feats of ocean navigation in the history of exploration. On an earlier expedition, into the Arctic with Captain William Parry during his 1821 attempt to find the Northwest Passage, your ships were stuck in ice for two winters. It was then that you first met Inuit, who tried your European name as *Croz-har*, but then settled on calling you Aglukkaq (Aglooka) — "He Who Takes Long Strides."

All told, through seven voyages, you have survived 10 full winters in far worse ships, trapped for weeks upon weeks in the ice of what felt like a frozen hell at the extremes of the planet. Each time, you have returned to great glory.

While you don't share an aristocratic background and might not be invited to formal tea in their mansions, the admirals of the Royal Navy had no choice but to recognize that the best guarantee this expedition will succeed is your knowledge and experience.

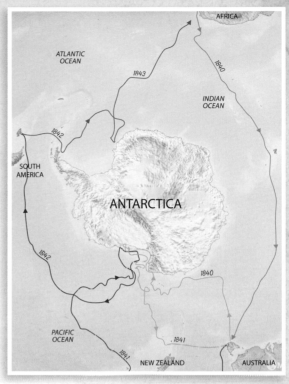

Crozier and Ross sailed these Antarctic routes in *Terror* and *Erebus* in 1841, breaking the record for farthest voyage south.

James Clark Ross, Royal Navy officer, nephew of Sir John Ross and Crozier's friend and fellow explorer

The *Erebus* and *Terror* in New Zealand, 1841, when Crozier first commanded the *Terror*. Painting by John Wilson Carmichael.

Erebus and Terror

John Franklin first inspected *Erebus* and *Terror* in 1840, during his time as lieutenant-governor of Van Diemen's Land, today known as the island of Tasmania, off the Australian coast. (It's also where Francis Crozier first met and fell in love with Franklin's niece, Sophia Cracroft, who stayed at the lieutenant-governor's opulent mansion.)

At that time, Crozier was captain of the *Terror*, constructed in 1813, and James Clark Ross was captain of the *Erebus*, built in 1826. The three-month stopover in Van Diemen's Land was part of their 1839–1843 expedition to the Antarctic to locate the South Pole.

The ships had been built to fire mortars, a type of cannon capable of sending 90 kg (200 lb.) loads of explosives farther than 3 km (2 mi.). To deal with such tremendous recoil, the ships were strongly built, with wide beams and an almost flat bottom to provide stability. Although this made them slow and difficult to maneuver, it also made them perfect for dangerous icy waters, since they would be able to withstand far more pressure from crushing ice than faster but less stable ships.

For Franklin's 1845 expedition, the *Erebus* and *Terror* were further modified with steam-powered engines, screw propellers, iron plating on the hulls and extra cross-planking across the decks to resist greater ice pressures. In short, the ships were as technologically advanced in their day as were the spaceships of the Apollo 11 program for the epic voyage to the moon some 12 decades later.

The Antarctic expedition was a massive success, both ships going farther south than any other ship in history. And during its earlier time as a mortar bomb ship, the *Terror* did add one other footnote to history.

In the War of 1812 between Great Britain and the United States, officers and crew of the *Terror* anchored the ship in the waters of Baltimore Harbor to bombard Fort McHenry day and night. An American lawyer was so inspired by the sight of the flags above the fort still waving at dawn that he put his feelings into the words of a poem he titled "The Defence of Fort M'Henry." Today we know that poem by a different title — "The Star-Spangled Banner." Indeed, it was the mortar fire from the *Terror* that Francis Scott Key famously described as "the rockets' red glare, the bombs bursting in air."

The man on deck beside you is your superior in rank, Sir John Franklin. Although Franklin has bungled previous Arctic expeditions, and some would argue that his social connections earned him his role as commander, you and the crew do respect the man and his experience as an explorer.

At this moment, Franklin is acknowledging the crowd's adoration and waving a brightly colored handkerchief at his wife and niece below on the docks.

Adding to your bitterness is that his niece, Sophia Cracroft, is the reason for your heartbreak. You are nearing 50 years of age and, after a lifetime as a bachelor, you were delighted to meet her through Franklin. You fell for Sophy and foolishly believed she might accept your marriage proposal based on your merits. Instead, she politely declined and yet again you discovered that without proper breeding, family and social graces, you will never be accepted into high society. You do have one hope, although a faint one. If the expedition is successful, your fame and possible promotion might be enough to impress her and gain her hand in marriage.

Captain Sir John Franklin, commander of the Franklin expedition

The prize will come at great cost. Of any man alive, you are fully aware of how horrible it will be to spend another winter — or longer — trying to survive the howling blizzards of the Arctic. Nor can you shake the premonition that this voyage, unlike the previous seven, is doomed. This feeling, something you expressed privately to a fellow officer after too much whiskey a few nights before, weighs down any hopes you might have.

While you fear that Franklin's overconfidence and bad decisions will prove your premonitions correct, one single danger awaits you that you cannot foresee, despite all your experience in the Arctic.

Steam tug towing a ship down the Thames

For as the tugboats begin to pull both ships away from the docks and into the current of the Thames, there is a man among the crowd who will prove as much an enemy to the expedition as the worst of an Arctic winter. Months from now, as dozens of your men face the horrible agony unleashed upon them because of his greed — or greed and incompetence? — he will be sitting in front of his cozy fireplace in his mansion, made wealthy through his business dealings with the Royal Navy. But you won't know of his betrayal until it is far too late.

As for you?

You are Francis Rawdon Moira Crozier — explorer, sailor and scientist. What lies ahead for you is far worse than any premonition of doom could foretell.

Apply Forensic Techniques to
Solve the Mystery

It was late spring 1950 in Denmark. At first, two men believed they had found a recent murder victim, with skin so fresh-looking that the face showed about a day's worth of stubble on the upper lip and chin.

The men had been cutting layers of peat moss to be used as fuel. Some 2 m (7 ft.) down into the peat, they discovered a body curled into a fetal position.

More bizarre, the victim's only clothing was a pointed cap made of sheepskin and wool, fastened below his chin by a strap, and a hide belt around his waist.

As for cause of death? That was obvious. There was a noose made from braided leather tight around his neck.

You are the forensic scientist invited to perform an autopsy, and you see that the rope left furrows at the side of the neck and under the chin. Hanging, you decide, and not strangulation, led to the mystery man's death.

Only 60 m (200 ft.) away, and 12 years earlier, a woman's body had also been found in peat, wrapped in a sheepskin cape. Her death had also apparently been caused by hanging.

Was this the work of a weird killer who dressed his victims in apparel from centuries before?

As a forensic scientist, you understand the location of both bodies in the peat is significant. How do you apply forensic techniques to decide this is not the work of a modern serial killer?

Answer at end of the chapter.

THE SEARCH THEN : Solemn Promise

Sir John Ross,
May 1845: London, England

Eleven days before the departure, the Admiralty of the Royal Navy — high-ranking officers who formed a commission and made joint decisions for the entire navy — hosted a formal reception for the officers of the *Erebus* and *Terror*. The Admiralty had given Franklin's expedition their blessing and were enjoying all the praise heaped upon them by newspapers.

Despite the spirit of optimism at this reception, it came with what was likely the first public discussion of the possible need for a search party for the expedition.

That's because there was a small group of men in the room not quite so enthusiastic. This was the Arctic Council, made up of surviving commanders of unsuccessful attempts to conquer the Northwest Passage by ship: Sir William Parry, 55 years old, four attempts; Sir George Back, 49 years old, two attempts, one by sea and one by land; and Sir John Ross, nearing retirement at 68 years old, two attempts.

During those eight attempts, over a series of winters, a total of 12 men had died, a number considered astoundingly high. It was inconceivable, of course, that the entire crews of the *Terror* and *Erebus* might perish, let alone never be found.

Sir William Edward Parry

Sir George Back

Sir John Ross

With their collective experience in the north, those three commanders were less certain than the Admiralty that the *Erebus* and *Terror*, outfitted with steel-plated hulls and modern engines, would survive the worst of the Arctic conditions.

Surely, given these previous challenges, the Admiralty and

Franklin himself understood that it would be no easy task to find the passage? Yet it was only John Ross who gave voice to any doubts on record from that evening. He was close friends with Franklin. Some 30 years earlier, Ross had been a captain and Franklin a lieutenant on their failed attempt to sail to the North Pole in an expedition with four ships.

While the Admiralty celebrated with toasts to success, Ross asked his friend a series of challenging questions.

An artist's depiction of the collision of *Erebus* and *Terror* in Antarctic waters, March 1842, from James Clark Ross's *A Voyage of Discovery and Research in the Southern and Antarctic Regions*. The ships were forced into each other to avoid crashing into an iceberg that suddenly appeared out of nowhere.

Why was Franklin taking 134 men?

John Ross's crew — forced to abandon their ship *Victory* during their 1829 voyage — had been only 23.

Why were the ships so big?

The waters were uncharted and the depths unpredictable. Earlier ships — Parry's *Fury* and Ross's *Victory*, at half the size — had still proven too large to get through waters without running aground.

Why the reliance on steam engines?

Although Ross had previously supported steam power, on his 1829–1833 expedition it had proved unreliable. He argued that provisions were the most important factor, and the considerable space steam engines and coal took in the ships' holds should not be the priority.

Aside from message canisters with preprinted notes to be dropped at sea or on shore to guide searchers, why were there no extensive emergency plans in case of trouble?

Ross expected that Franklin would have a route laid out in case men needed to escape the Arctic on foot — and a route for searchers. Ross also expected that Franklin would anchor occasionally to leave behind stacks of food and equipment in case the ships — or men on foot — needed to retrace their route. Franklin did not share all of those concerns, confident that with the new technology of canned foods, there was no danger the men would ever starve. Ross could hardly believe Franklin's shortsightedness. Then and there, at the Admiralty reception in May 1845, Ross made a solemn promise. If there had been no word from Franklin by February of 1847, Ross himself would lead the search party to rescue him.

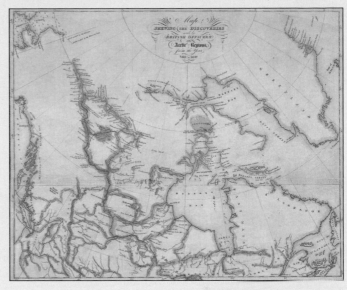

Map Shewing the Discoveries Made by British Officers in the Arctic Regions, from the Year 1818 to 1826, from Franklin's *Narrative of a Second Expedition to the Shores of the Polar Sea*. In this earlier expedition, Franklin traveled inland from Lake Superior to the Arctic Sea.

The irony was that neither Franklin nor Ross, both experienced explorers, heeded one piece of advice that might have changed the course of the expedition. It came from the man who would command the *Erebus* under Franklin, Captain James Fitzjames. Because the canned provisions came from a new supplier, Fitzjames had suggested that every tenth case be examined before the ships departed.

But time was too short, and Franklin brushed off the suggestion.

Elsewhere at the time ...

The Stamped Stamp

With massive media attention breathlessly focused on the future success of Franklin's expedition, other events in the world seemed to take place much more quietly. For example, in 1845, some postmasters in the United States finally began to adopt something that the United Kingdom of Great Britain and Ireland had introduced in May 1840: postage stamps.

Hacking isn't new to this generation. When that first stamp was released, post office officials already anticipated that people would try to game the system by peeling stamps off a delivered envelope to use that stamp again. Those wavy lines inked onto the stamps? Yup. Called "postmarking."

OF SHIPS AND MEN : A Patient Hunter

Louie Kamookak,
August 1979: Terror Bay, King William Island

"Three elders told me: If you travel on King William Island, do not ever travel alone because there's bad spirits there. I think they're referring to the Franklin men ..."

— Louie Kamookak

In late summer, far north of where trees grow, ice floes drift brilliant white in the calm blue waters named nearly a century earlier in honor of HMS *Terror*. From the shoreline of Terror Bay (Amitruq) this time of year on the southwestern side of King William Island (Qikiqtaq), it's difficult to imagine great sheets of ice jammed in at all angles, pushed into the shoreline by the currents of the Arctic Ocean.

Summer exposes the island for what it is: essentially an Arctic desert with gravel instead of sand. No trees. Little vegetation.

It was here, overlooking the waters of Terror Bay, that Louie Kamookak found an old rope and a piece of wood inside a circle of stones. Because of his Inuit heritage, passed on by the Nattilingmiut who had roamed this island for centuries, Kamookak knew he was looking at an old Inuit tent ring.

Kamookak, a large man with rounded shoulders and a rounded face, had been walking the gravel bars as part of his lifelong dedication to solving the mystery of the fate of the Franklin expedition. During earlier searches, he had once turned over a rock to find the amulet belt of an Inuit shaman, a spiritual healer. Next to notched pieces of bone were pocket scissors, now rusty, that looked like they might have come from a surgeon's case or a navy seaman's sewing kit.

Summer Tents of the Eskimaux, Igloolik, 1822, from William Parry's 1824 journal. Inuit tent rings are stones arranged in a circle to hold tent walls in place.

On this day at Terror Bay, it was the piece of wood that drew him. Far to the south, below the tree line, a piece of wood would have little significance. Here, it was a foreign material. Kamookak had little difficulty believing it was another clue to the fate of Franklin's expedition, a mystery shrouded in Arctic fog for more than a century already.

Barely 30 at the time, Kamookak had been hunting for clues since he first heard the name of Sir John Franklin in his final year at residential school, a place far away from his home in Gjoa Haven (Ursuqtuuq) on the eastern side of the island.

Taught by white teachers, forced to learn about subjects that had no relevance to him, sitting on uncomfortable bench seats, Kamookak had little interest in school. During his daydreams that took him out of the classroom, he was back on the land, camping in tents, listening to the stories of his great-grandmother Hu'mahuk. In passing down stories of their people, she was continuing Inuit oral tradition.

But that day in school, when he heard that Franklin had led white men who came from across the sea to the North, his curiosity surged, awakening him from his daydreams.

Hu'mahuk had told tales about those men! Her father had been among the Inuit who encountered *qaplunaaq*, the white men, who sailed massive wooden ships that towered far above the waters! Her father had found a butter knife from those men that he'd turned into an ice chisel! As a child, Hu'mahuk had walked by the grave of a mariner whose body had been buried beneath rocks by the beach, with musket balls and other items scattered near a large mound!

Since the day he'd heard Franklin's name, Kamookak couldn't stop thinking about the tales told to him by Hu'mahuk.

King William Island, Nunavut, in the Canadian Arctic Archipelago. It was first thought to be a peninsula and was known on maps as King William Land, even 20 years after it was discovered to be an island in 1834.

Louie Kamookak, teacher and Inuit historian, at Peabody Point on King William Island in 2015

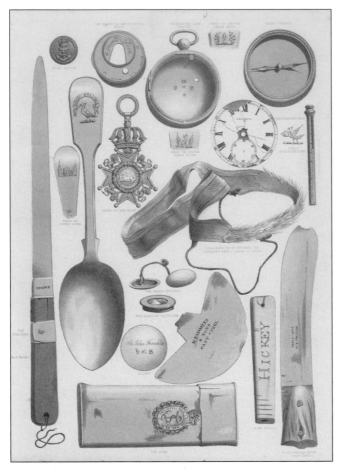

An illustration of objects left behind by the Franklin expedition

It became an obsession that he never lost all through his years into adulthood. For Kamookak, any physical clues he could find were of value. Yet far more important to him than objects like butter knives and pocket scissors and pieces of wood from the abandoned ships were the tales told by his people, the last known to have any encounters with the officers and crew.

Kamookak believed that the Nattilingmiut — Inuit who live west of Hudson Bay on the Arctic coast — knew what happened to *Erebus* and *Terror* and the officers and crew who, to the rest of the world, had simply disappeared.

Kamookak was well-suited to unravel this mystery. He lived on the land; he spoke the language. And unlike the "outsiders" who could not sort out good information from bad, he trusted Inuit oral tradition.

Outsiders couldn't puzzle out locations based on traditional Inuit names for places.

Outsiders couldn't sit for long hours with elders to gently tease out more details from the stories passed along from one generation to the next.

Inuit had tales about the ships. About a strange small boat with tubes on its sides to hold air. About blackened men. About four survivors and a dog that roamed the island. And about one of those survivors, a white man they named Aglukkaq, "He Who Takes Long Strides."

Neptune, a gift from Lady Franklin to the crew of Sir John Franklin's Arctic expedition, was one of three pet animals that sailed on board HMS *Erebus*.

After years upon years of roaming the island, of meeting with elders, of looking at maps, of going through Inuit tales recorded by outsiders, Kamookak put stock in his great-grandmother's stories. He wondered if the place to look for the ships was in an area that outsiders called Erebus Bay, where archaeologists had found items from the expedition, such as a bone toothbrush and sailors' buttons.

And underlying the search — for Kamookak, historians and forensic scientists all investigating a mystery more than a century old — was one central question.

How and why did the expedition fail so badly?

This canister found in a cairn on King William Island contained a 138-word message.

Mystery SOLVED

Congratulations if you understood that a combination of acid and the lack of oxygen in peat moss, plus Denmark's cold climate, made an excellent burial site for preserving bodies.

Through radiocarbon dating, you can conclude that although the skin looks fresh, this man was buried in the peat moss over 2000 years earlier.

By noting the carefully arranged position of the body, you are also able to determine that Tollund Man — as he is now known to the world — did die by hanging, but was most likely a victim of a ritual human sacrifice, just like Elling Woman, found nearby.

Bog body Tollund Man

EPISODE TWO
Smooth Sailing

TIMELINE

MAY 1845: THE DOCKS AT GREENHITHE, THAMES RIVER, LONDON, ENGLAND

JULY 1845: DISKO BAY, GREENLAND

AUGUST TO SEPTEMBER 1845: LANCASTER SOUND

SEPTEMBER 1845 TO AUGUST 1846: BEECHEY ISLAND

AUGUST TO SEPTEMBER 1846: PEEL SOUND AND FRANKLIN STRAIT

SEPTEMBER 1846: KING WILLIAM ISLAND

SEPTEMBER 1846 TO JUNE 1847: LAT 70°05' N, LONG 98°23' W

JUNE 1847 TO APRIL 1848: SHIPS LOCKED IN ICE

AUGUST 1848: BOOTH POINT, KING WILLIAM ISLAND

SEPTEMBER 1848: MONTREAL ISLAND, MOUTH OF THE BACK RIVER

HUDSON BAY

NORTH AMERICA

CANADA

PACIFIC OCEAN

UNITED STATES

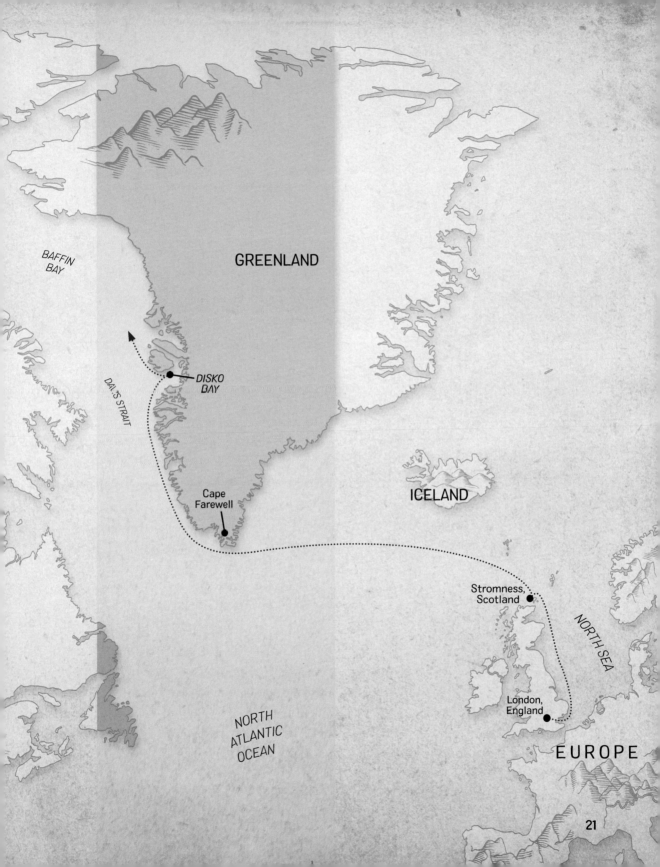

BAFFIN
BAY

GREENLAND

DAVIS STRAIT

DISKO
BAY

Cape
Farewell

ICELAND

Stromness,
Scotland

NORTH SEA

London,
England

NORTH
ATLANTIC
OCEAN

EUROPE

YOUR EXPEDITION : Last Words

July 1845: Disko Bay, Greenland

It is July 12. You sit at your writing desk in your cramped officer's cabin belowdecks of the anchored *Terror*, your ship swaying slightly in the calm waters of Disko Bay (Qeqertarsuaq Tunua) off the western coast of Greenland. At this time of year, enough daylight comes from the stern gallery windows and a skylight that you do not need a lamp to see your handwriting as you compose a letter to your friend and fellow explorer James Clark Ross.

Island of Disco and Icebergs, from John Ross's A Voyage of Discovery, Made under the Orders of the Admiralty, in His Majesty's Ships Isabella *and* Alexander, *1819*

My dear James, I cannot allow Transport to leave without writing you a line, altho' I have little to say and our many details keep me in anything but a fit mood for letter writing …

Ross, of anyone, would understand what you face. You and Ross narrowly escaped death in the Antarctic storms during the expedition that you shared years earlier — he as captain of the *Erebus*, and you as captain of the *Terror*.

All things are going well and quietly but we are I fear sadly late —

As you write, the smell of blood reaches you through the hatch, along with the bellows of oxen as they face slaughter on the deck of *Barretto Junior*, a transport ship anchored nearby. It followed *Erebus* and *Terror* here to a Danish whaling station. It is carrying masses of supplies so that both ships were not overloaded for the treacherous North Atlantic crossing and to replace supplies used during the crossing.

Your crew will load the oxen carcasses and tons of provisions into the lower holds of both ships, at the same time replenishing coal supplies to ensure there is enough coal to fire the engines when you cannot use the sails. *Barretto Junior* will return to England, while you sail north into a growing pack of ice.

Danish Whaling Station, by Abraham Speeck, 1634. By the eighteenth century, the whaling industry had made Denmark and the Netherlands hugely wealthy. Whales were usually harpooned close to shore and then towed in small boats to land. There, whalers cut off their blubber, heated it in great cauldrons and poured the precious extracted oil into barrels to go back on the ships. Whale oil was used for lamp fuel, candle wax and soap; whalebones were used in ladies' corsets and umbrellas; and ambergris, from the intestines of whales, was used in perfumes.

Moving all of those supplies from one ship to the other — even you wonder where it can fit in the already stuffed lower hold — will take at least a week, precious time in a season that is already too short. Your anxiousness eats at you, especially after you speak with the Danish whalers. You remark on your latest concern in your letter.

From what we can learn the weather here has been very severe with much Easterly wind …

A few weeks earlier, you and your officers and crew had rounded Cape Farewell, the southernmost tip of Greenland.

Many of them had gasped at their first glimpse of the Arctic world. The ice along the coastline was a glacier more than 1.6 km (1 mi.) high, taller than Ben Nevis, the highest mountain in Scotland, for as far as the eye could see. The cold of the ice creates its own climate system, sending the constant roar of a freezing wind out to sea.

To reach Disko Bay, you continued north and upwind along Greenland's west coast into the Davis Strait, wishing the ships could be faster, but knowing that the modifications that make it slower have also made it safer for travel in ice pack.

Whale oil lantern

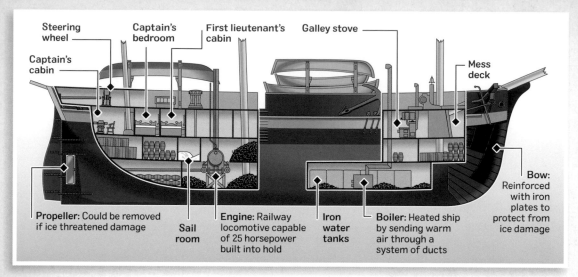

Steering wheel

Captain's bedroom

First lieutenant's cabin

Galley stove

Captain's cabin

Mess deck

Propeller: Could be removed if ice threatened damage

Sail room

Engine: Railway locomotive capable of 25 horsepower built into hold

Iron water tanks

Boiler: Heated ship by sending warm air through a system of ducts

Bow: Reinforced with iron plates to protect from ice damage

This cutaway view of the HMS *Erebus* shows the vast amount of space taken up by food, coal and other provisions meant to last an expedition of three years.

Like the *Erebus*, the *Terror* has had its hull doubled and sheathed with plates of iron. Belowdecks of each is a steam engine and tons upon tons of coal, added to tons upon tons of provisions: more than 10 400 kg (23 000 lb.) of sugar for the almost sacred British tradition of tea, 14 617 kg (32 224 lb.) of beef and almost an equal amount of pork. Added to this is 14 969 kg (33 000 lb.) of boiled and roast beef and mutton, veal and ox-cheek preserved by the latest technology — canned food. With canned vegetables, including potatoes, carrots and parsnips, each crew member would receive about a pint of soup a day, seasoned with 90 kg (200 lb.) of pepper; 2636 L (580 imp. gal.) of pickled cabbage, onions and walnuts; 453 kg (1000 lb.) of mustard; and 77 kg (170 lb.) of cranberries.

You are worried about ice conditions in Baffin Bay and want to get into Lancaster Sound at the earliest opportunity.

What I fear is that from our being so late we shall have no time to look round and judge for our selves, but blunder into the Ice and make a second 1824 of it.

Yes. In 1824, you and James Clark Ross, the man you are now writing to, had voyaged north with William Parry to explore the waters ahead of you. An early winter stopped your progress. All told, that expedition was a disaster, as you were forced to abandon your mission at the west end of Baffin Island, where one of your ships was crushed by the ice pack.

Sir John Franklin — The Best Choice?

The expedition's future challenges were understood, but the prize to be gained was seen as well worth the investment.

A route across the top of the world would cut weeks off the sailing time it took to voyage round the dangerous waters at the tip of South America. Sir John Barrow, Second Secretary to the Admiralty, wanted the glory of the discovery of that northern passage to go to Britain's Royal Navy.

It would require navigating the *Erebus* and *Terror* through only partially charted Arctic waters in an imperfectly known maze of islands, dead-end inlets and pack ice that could snap shut like a jaw overnight, then open again unexpectedly a day or a week or a month later.

Furthermore, although Royal Navy explorers routinely recorded depths, not all of these waters had yet been mapped for depth. With large and heavily laden ships, there was a constant danger of grounding.

Barrow needed to convince Parliament that, despite the earlier attempts that had resulted in lost ships, these were challenges that the right ships, officers and crew could overcome. Armed with Britain's new technology and scientific prowess, they could all but guarantee Britain the glory.

It would take a heroic figure as a commander to fire up public and parliamentary support for yet another search for the Northwest Passage. On the one hand, Sir John Franklin was perfect. His father was a merchant descended from a line of country gentlemen, and he was married to a woman with strong connections.

On the other hand, although certainly competent, Franklin was an old man in Barrow's eyes. Barrow had sent Franklin north three times already, but not everyone considered those expeditions successes. While serving as lieutenant-governor of Van Diemen's Land, Franklin faced complex challenges there, including having to set up a new convict labor system in a colony suffering from financial depression. As well, some of his superiors thought he was too "sensitive" and his wife had too much influence on policy decisions. Eventually, after six years, he was recalled to Britain. It was a blow to his reputation. There were reasons Barrow had not given Franklin any kind of significant assignment in 16 years.

Franklin's wife, Lady Franklin, refused to let her husband's failures stand in the way of landing him this high-profile role. She used her influence in as many places as possible until everyone but Barrow believed in Franklin as commander.

Eventually Barrow offered Franklin the position of leader of the expedition. With Francis Crozier as captain of the *Terror* and James Fitzjames commanding the *Erebus*, the voyage looked like it was in safe hands.

The Fury *Grounded on Fury Beach,* from William Edward Parry's *Journal of a Third Voyage for the Discovery of a North-West Passage,* 1826

As you pause with your pen above paper, thoughts of that unfortunate trip with Ross and Parry in 1824 lead you to mentally review the task set before Franklin by Sir John Barrow, Second Secretary of the Admiralty. Your orders are to proceed to Greenland, followed by ships carrying additional coal and supplies. Find anchorage and transfer the provisions onto the *Erebus* and *Terror.* That initial stage of your mission is almost complete. Next, cross Baffin Bay and travel 1450 km (900 mi.) west through Lancaster Sound to Barrow Strait,

Detail from *Discoveries of Captains Ross, Parry and Franklin in the Arctic Regions in 1818, 1819, 1820, 1821 and 1822.* The Franklin Expedition relied on the maps and reports of these early explorers, but much was still unknown in 1845. In this historical map, Greenland, Baffin Bay, Lancaster Sound and the Barrow Strait are all shown, but there is no passage to the Bering Strait and the Pacific Ocean.

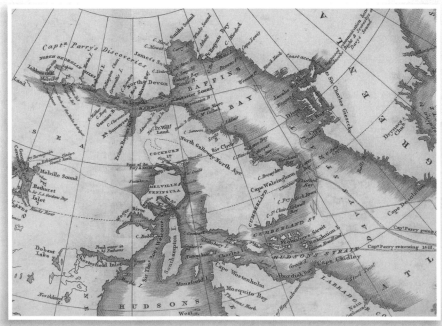

named for Sir John himself. Venture south into unknown waters to hit the mainland of North America. Then sail and steam west along the coastline to the Bering Strait and into the Pacific, all the while recording valuable geomagnetic observations.

On the existing nautical charts, this looks simple. Certainly there are blank spots remaining to be mapped, but the Northwest Passage itself appears to be only 800 km (500 mi.) from east to west. While Franklin has prepared to spend a winter in ice, the optimistic view is that even if heavier-than-expected ice packs slowed their pace, in good conditions, the ships could easily cover 800 km to reach the Bering Strait in a matter of weeks.

HMS *Terror* was sent to explore the North American shore west of Hudson Bay in 1836, but became trapped by ice near Southampton Island, at the north end of Hudson Bay, for more than 10 months under the command of George Back. By the time the ship limped back home across the Atlantic, it was badly damaged and needed extensive repairs.

You want to share Franklin's optimism. Yet because of the 1824 expedition you worry. You know that the ice pack can crush these ships as if they were made of paper. You know that coastlines are rarely straight, and that 800 km as the crow flies could easily be double that distance through a maze of islands.

Your anxiety is worsened by the yearning you have for the woman you love, the one who spurned you. Franklin's constant invitations to dine with him in his spacious cabin on the *Erebus* are only reminders of your sorrow.

James dear I am sadly alone, not a soul have I in either ship that I can go and talk to. "No congenial spirit as it were." I am generally busy but it is after all a very hermit like life — Well my dear friend, I know not what else I can say to you — I feel that I am not in spirits for wintering but in truth I am sadly lonely.

You sign the letter and fold it and seal it with wax. The transport ship will take your mail, and the mail of all the officers and crew, back to England. It will also leave with a few men you have decided are unfit for the voyage.

As you leave your quarters to move to the upper deck and supervise the loading of provisions, you have no idea that your letter will be the last written words you send back to England.

Franklin's cabin in the *Erebus* was separate from his sleeping quarters.

Apply Forensic Techniques to
Solve the Mystery

In 1901, members of an expedition in Siberia found a frozen male mammoth. The extreme Arctic cold preserves these animals so well that often the flesh is still pink and blood can be found inside the veins.

In this case, the mammoth was such a good specimen that it still had grass in its mouth. The expedition transported the prize mammoth to St. Petersburg, where the beast's skin and bones were put on display.

And the meat? The meat, it was reported, was served at a banquet, where one guest enthusiastically wrote that "all the learned guests declared [it] was agreeable to the taste, and not much tougher than some of the sirloin furnished by butchers of today."

Yet, as a forensic scientist familiar with Arctic conditions, you wonder if perhaps those guests were overeager to believe that what they had been served came from a mammoth. What do you know that leads you to your conclusion?

Answer at end of the chapter.

THE SEARCH THEN :
The Man Who Ate His Boots
Sir John Richardson,
August 1845: London, England

In August, the transport *Barretto Junior* returned to London from Greenland carrying five crew who had been discharged, along with letters home from the remaining 129 officers and crew.

It was natural for Sir John Franklin to include a letter to Sir John Richardson, his friend and fellow Arctic explorer. Decades earlier, over the course of two Arctic expeditions, Franklin and Richardson had surveyed more than 2900 km (1800 mi.) of previously unmapped coastline.

That's why Richardson, of all people, would have also understood all the reasons why Franklin emphasized the quantity of provisions aboard the ship.

First, he would have shared Franklin's relief that in the final days before departure, the relatively unknown contractor Stephan Goldner had delivered on his brash promise to the Admiralty. Only two days before departure from the docks at Greenhithe, his canning company had at last begun to deliver tons of canned foods. Filling the ships had delayed departure by eight days, but this seemed like a minor transgression. Yes, some of the cans were larger than promised, but Goldner had explained that filling the smaller cans agreed to in his contract had been taking too much time. Larger cans were more efficient in terms of labor, and necessary to meet the Admiralty's deadline. With little grumbling, his excuses were accepted, and he would earn more contracts for future expeditions, including for ships sent out years later to search for the *Terror* and *Erebus*.

Sir John Richardson, Scottish surgeon, naturalist and Arctic explorer

John Richardson traveled with Franklin on his second Arctic expedition in 1826. Richardson successfully journeyed east to the Coppermine River using these small but oceanworthy boats, the *Dolphin* and *Union*.

Delayed or not, cans too large or not, for the first time in history, an expedition of this nature would be able to depart with no concerns about starvation. So Franklin assured Richardson with his comment that "we can, without apprehension remain a second winter."

Franklin's relief at the secured provisions would have been significant to Richardson for a second reason. During one of Franklin's expeditions to the Arctic, from 1819 to 1822 — when Franklin was supposed to complete the overland voyage to meet with William Parry and Francis Crozier, who were in ships stuck in pack ice — food ran so low that the men began eating caribou skins embedded with fly maggots that would explode with a salty milky fluid when crunched between teeth. Under Franklin's leadership, 11 of 20 men died, most dying from starvation, and Franklin missed the rendezvous. Worse, when the caribou skins were gone, Franklin and the survivors of his team were reduced to eating shoe leather and caribou droppings. It had earned him a reputation in the newspapers as "the man who ate his boots."

Although the story accurately portrayed Franklin in a heroic light, the difficulties of his posting as lieutenant-governor of Van Diemen's Land, the Australian island colony, and the manner of his leaving that position opened the door to criticism for how he had handled previous challenges.

Indeed, in reading a letter from his friend, Richardson would have been acutely conscious of the fact that Franklin

A leather seaboot from the 1845 expedition was found in Starvation Cove in the late 1870s.

had not been the Navy's first choice for command of this expedition. Moreover, at 59 years of age, Franklin was no longer in his prime.

Richardson would have also known that the political push — including Lady Franklin's lobbying — to install Franklin as commander succeeded not necessarily because of the Admiralty's confidence in Franklin, but in the belief that with 500 ships and charts of nearly every explorable part of the world, the Royal Navy was a global empire. Bolstering this confidence were achievements resulting from England's Industrial Revolution over the previous few decades — blast furnaces and steam engines among them. Another large part of the Admiralty's complacency came from the knowledge that the well-provisioned expedition would be self-sufficient for years. No one would starve.

Thus, Sir John Franklin had provided the necessary figurehead to guarantee that Parliament voted in favor of the massive funding needed, while Francis Crozier, as second-in-command, was seen as the insurance for the success of the voyage.

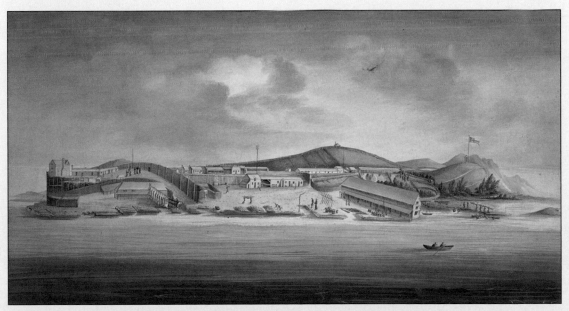

The Macquarie Harbour settlement, in Van Dieman's Land, 1833, a few years before Franklin arrived. Watercolor painting by William Buelow Gould.

In short, from the Admiralty's perspective, it would be simply a matter of waiting until the *Erebus* and *Terror* emerged on the Pacific side of the Northwest Passage.

After all, with a combination of new Industrial Revolution technology, Crozier and Fitzjames — two of the most experienced and successful Arctic explorers in history — on board, and enough canned food for years, how could Franklin's expedition not succeed?

Who could have predicted that, years later, Sir John Richardson would be sent back into the Arctic to search for his friend?

Elsewhere at the time ...

Massive Unemployment Because of a Simple Machine That Saved Work?

Public excitement about the expedition, stirred up by the press, was ebbing. Most expected the next blitz of news to happen when both ships emerged safely in the Pacific. That left room in the newspapers for articles about a demonstration held in Boston at that time.

Of significance to the demonstration were events in France in 1830, when a tailor named Barthélemy Thimonnier nearly died at the hands of a group of other tailors who burned down his garment factory. They feared unemployment because of a machine he'd invented to replace hand sewing.

It wasn't until 1845 that the modern sewing machine was introduced to the world, by Elias Howe in Boston. Howe arranged a demonstration, a race of his machine against five speedy seamstresses.

The first patented lockstitch sewing machine, invented by Elias Howe in 1845 and patented in 1846

The machine worked at an incredible pace of 250 stitches per minute, when the most skilled hand-stitchers could do only 50. Ironically, Howe didn't make his fortune with the machine itself, but by suing competitors who infringed on his patent.

OF SHIPS AND MEN : A Bowl of China

Owen Beattie, August 1981,
Starvation Cove, King William Island

"After a painstaking, finger-numbing search, Beattie's team found human bones with knife marks and skulls with no faces."

— From Margaret Atwood's foreword to *Frozen in Time: The Fate of the Franklin Expedition*, by Owen Beattie and John Geiger

By 1981, more than 13 decades had passed since the Royal Navy first sent out searchers. Since then, a staggering 36 expeditions of polar explorers had gone in search of the fate of the *Erebus* and *Terror*. They'd had many tantalizing questions but few satisfactory answers.

What had been known for decades was that after making landfall on King William Island in 1848, officers and crew had begun marching south. In 1869, American journalist Charles Francis Hall, during his search for the fate of the Franklin expedition, had learned from Inuit that some of the last survivors had crossed a spit of land farther south, on their way to Starvation Cove. Inuit called this place Kung-e-ark-le ar-u, and knew it was here "that a white man had been buried."

In 1869, Inuit had pointed out this spot to Hall, but it was too snow-covered for him to closely examine the burial place. Still, Hall found the body believed to be that of Lieutenant Henry LeVesconte, later identified as Harry Goodsir, in part based on gold tooth fillings. So he erected a monument and made notes of its location.

Where were the resting places of the ships? Why would the sailors abandon their ships when that was their best shelter? Why would they try to go south by land when anyone looking for them would have come from the north? And why — with so many weapons and supplies — had no one survived to tell the outside world the fate of the long-disappeared expedition?

Nearly 120 years later, Owen Beattie, a Canadian professor of anthropology, took up the challenge. Beattie believed that if he could find any of the bones of that long-dead "white man," his specialized knowledge of human skeletal biology and his forensic skills might answer some of those questions.

Anthropologist Owen Beattie in 2014

Charles Francis Hall, American journalist and Arctic explorer, with Inuit interpreters Taqulittuq (Tookoolito) and Ipirvik (Ebierbing)

Beattie's quest took him to King William Island, the home of Louie Kamookak, that land of mud and limestone and ice-water lakes, where vegetation of any kind is almost nonexistent.

To get there, Beattie flew by commercial jet from his home in Edmonton, Alberta, to Yellowknife, in the Northwest Territories of Canada. From there, a much smaller plane took him hours to the north and east, to Resolute, a community of fewer than 200 people.

There, he picked up supplies that would mean the difference between life and death. As important as food and tents were a shortwave radio, a rifle and a shotgun. Polar bears, after all, consider humans just as much prey as they do the seals that they stalk among the ice floes in the water beyond the beach.

From Resolute, it was still more hours in the air, in a Twin Otter large enough only for his supplies and the rest of his team of university students helping with the search. They flew south and east, to the Inuit community of Gjoa Haven, Kamookak's

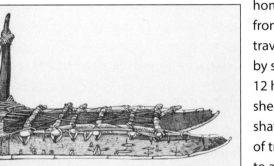

In February 1866, Hall found this very heavy Inuit sledge made from the jawbone of a whale, with runners that were 3.7 m (12 ft.) long. From the *Narrative of the Second Arctic Expedition made by Charles F. Hall: His Voyage to Repulse Bay, Sledge Journeys to the Straits of Fury and Hecla and to King William's Land, and Residence among the Eskimos, during the Years 1864-'69.*

home. Yet more journey stretched in front of them — none of it as easy as travel by air. Local hunters took them by snowmobiles to the west. It was 12 hours over hillocks, 12 hours over sheets of ice folded up like land shattered by an earthquake, 12 hours of trusting that the guides knew how to avoid the places on the Arctic Ocean where the ice is so thin that snowmobiles and sleds would break through, 12 hours of knowing that if they plunged into the water, even if they managed to haul themselves out again, they would freeze to death before anyone could start a fire or set up a heated shelter.

Difficult as their travel was with snowmobiles, it made it incomprehensible that anyone would ever attempt a journey like this, lost and starving, dragging heavy sleds to what they must have hoped was rescue.

All of the challenges of this modern journey would be rewarded if somehow they managed to locate those human remains Hall had been told of more than a century earlier, remains that had seemingly vanished. Beattie's hopes were raised when, on the second day of the search, someone on the team shouted and lifted something from the gravel beach.

The discovery looked like a broken bowl of china. It was brown on one side where it was exposed to the elements, bone white on the underside.

That's when Beattie's hope turned to the elation of success.

Because he was a forensic scientist, Beattie knew the color was bone white in a literal sense. It was a piece of a human skull, the first of the bones that the team would unearth during their time there. They had discovered the remains of a sailor from the long-lost expedition.

For an archaeologist or historian, only the location of those bones would have significance. For a forensic scientist like Beattie, however, those bones, when closely examined, showed patterns — patterns that Beattie began to fear pointed to a horrible truth about the death of the man.

The skull appeared to have been broken deliberately. On a right thigh bone, Beattie found three parallel grooves that could have been made only by a metal implement, like a knife.

For what terrible reason were those marks there?

William Skinner and Paddy Gibson discovered skulls of members of the Franklin expedition on King William Island in 1945 and took this photo before they buried them again.

 # Mystery SOLVED

Congratulations if you concluded that the organizers of the banquet misrepresented the meal. Yes, they were indeed serving sirloin instead of mammoth.

As a forensic scientist, you are aware of something called "grave wax," which is more technically known as adipocere. This is an organic soap of sorts, caused when a type of bacteria breaks down the body fat of corpses, especially bodies found in cool and wet conditions.

It is almost certain that the same rancid substance would be produced in a mammoth body.

Even without the presence of adipocere, ice crystals would have formed in the mammoth's muscle tissues. Once defrosted, the muscle would have turned into an unappetizing goo, as proven by a Russian paleontologist who tried to fry actual mammoth meat and ended up with a liquid that smelled horrible.

EPISODE
THREE
Arktos

● LANCASTER SOUND

BAFFIN
ISLAND

TIMELINE

MAY 1845: THE DOCKS AT GREENHITHE, THAMES RIVER, LONDON, ENGLAND

JULY 1845: DISKO BAY, GREENLAND

AUGUST TO SEPTEMBER 1845: LANCASTER SOUND

SEPTEMBER 1845 TO AUGUST 1846: BEECHEY ISLAND

AUGUST TO SEPTEMBER 1846: PEEL SOUND AND FRANKLIN STRAIT

SEPTEMBER 1846: KING WILLIAM ISLAND

SEPTEMBER 1846 TO JUNE 1847: LAT 70°05' N, LONG 98°23' W

JUNE 1847 TO APRIL 1848: SHIPS LOCKED IN ICE

AUGUST 1848: BOOTH POINT, KING WILLIAM ISLAND

SEPTEMBER 1848: MONTREAL ISLAND, MOUTH OF THE BACK RIVER

HUDSON
BAY

NORTH
AMERICA

CANADA

PACIFIC
OCEAN

UNITED STATES

BAFFIN
BAY

GREENLAND

DAVIS STRAIT

*DISKO
BAY*

Cape
Farewell

ICELAND

Stromness,
Scotland

NORTH SEA

NORTH
ATLANTIC
OCEAN

London,
England

EUROPE

WELLINGTON
CHANNEL

CORNWALLIS
ISLAND

DEVON ISLAND
●BEECHEY ISLAND

LANCASTER SOUND

SOMERSET
ISLAND

YOUR EXPEDITION : Icy Tomb

August to September 1845:
Lancaster Sound

"Do not get over anxious about us if we do no return in the time you have fixed upon. Be earnest in prayers for us as I will be for you & yours. Give my affectionate regards to all assisting you and believe me ever yours."

— Sir John Franklin, writing to his sister Isabella Cracroft

You stand at the rails on deck, breeze over your shoulder, happy to be ignored by crew members in constant motion around you. By now, it is known that you are almost a hermit, speaking only to give orders, never to make idle conversation.

You hold in your hand a cylinder of tinned iron about the size of a small spyglass, collapsed. One of your tasks is to note the time and location of the ships on a preprinted form, then seal it inside the cylinder. The form has instructions in English, French, German, Spanish and Danish for the finder to forward the cylinder to the Secretary of the Admiralty in London or the nearest British consul. Any that are found will help the Royal Navy understand Arctic Ocean currents or, unlikely as it seems, increase the chances of tracking the expedition if needed.

You fling the cylinder and your eyes trace the arc as it rises against a blue sky, then falls against the background of waves. It splashes, bobs and disappears as the ship slides away.

You glance across the aquamarine water at the *Erebus* and see your counterpart, James Fitzjames, on deck, taking measurements with a dip circle, which is essentially a magnetic needle mounted in the center of a circle. Not all the magnetic lines are aligned with the surface of the Earth — in some places it dips down and in other places tilts up. Charting the magnetic field globally is important for navigation and is the primary scientific purpose of the expedition. Indeed, Franklin is also an accomplished magnetic scientist and that probably influenced the Admiralty's decision to make him commander.

This is a bitter reminder of the politics behind the expedition. You have been consigned to dropping notes that will likely never be found. Fitzjames is taking magnetic measurements, but you are the one so good at that science

A dip circle measures the angle between the horizon and the Earth's magnetic field. This dip circle was found near Victory Point, King William Island, in 1859.

that in 1843, shortly after your highly successful Antarctic expedition with James Clark Ross, you were elected a Fellow of the Royal Society in the field of magnetism. On that journey, in addition to carrying out your naval duties, you acted as a scientist and researcher, making observations not only on magnetic readings, but also on ocean currents, weather and zoological sightings.

As a scientific body, the Royal Society is so exclusive it allows only 22 new members per year. Those who elected you were considered the elites of their fields, and among them were also the highest-ranking officials of the Admiralty.

Yet when it came to this expedition, less than two years later, the Admiralty gave this responsibility to Fitzjames, who has much less experience than you. Worse, from your perspective, the Admiralty gave Fitzjames control over the selection of officers and crew for this expedition. You would have chosen men experienced in ice and recruited from whaling fleets. Fitzjames had drawn from men he sailed with.

Although you are hurt that the younger man with no Arctic experience was favored, you are not surprised. Fitzjames, whose best friend is Sir John Barrow's son, had friends in the right places. You suffer from your Irish background. Fitzjames is handsome and charismatic and witty. You are silent and often appear sullen. Fitzjames enjoys cozying up for dinners with Franklin; you repeatedly find excuses to decline a short trip by rowboat to the *Erebus* to join them.

James Fitzjames, commander of the *Erebus*, entered the Royal Navy at the age of 12.

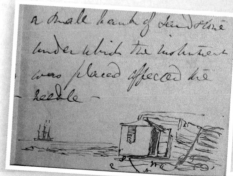

Arctic explorers set up magnetic stations, or observatories, to measure geomagnetic fields. In June 1845, Fitzjames sketched a magnetic station with HMS *Erebus* in the background (above, right). Some were constructed of blocks of snow, like igloos.

Keeping a lookout from the crow's nest

Now, as the sails are filled with a wind that has pushed you almost through Baffin Bay — the treacherous ice-filled waters west of Greenland — there is only the daily routine. Everyone knows their duties — surgeons, assistant surgeons, caulkers, sailmakers, cooks, stokers and able seamen, all listed by name on the ship's muster. All told, 129 officers and crew whose lives depend on the shared decisions that Franklin and you and Fitzjames will make as the ships proceed into the most hostile environment on the planet.

Some crew are on deck, scrubbing. Idle men cause trouble. Even with the deck clean, this is a daily chore.

Others climb like monkeys up the masts. There is constant inspection of sails. The rigging — the ropes that control the sails — needs daily repairs.

Below, other crew pump out water from the bilge. No matter how well built, every ship has leaks.

Your gaze takes in the blue serenity of open waters and the delightful — to the eyes — gleaming white dots scattered to the horizon. Up close, however, these are massive icebergs, a danger to be avoided at all costs. At night, high in the masts, crew take turns looking through the dimness to spot that danger.

A few weeks earlier, in late July, your ships had crossed paths with two whaling ships, *Prince of Wales* and *Enterprise,* anchored to the side of an iceberg. Their crew had been there long enough to build an observatory on top of the iceberg to scout the fastest route through the ice. They had also taken the opportunity from there to shoot hundreds of diving seabirds, called auks, salting them down and putting them in barrels for winter provisions.

These sailors will be the last Europeans to see any of your officers and crew.

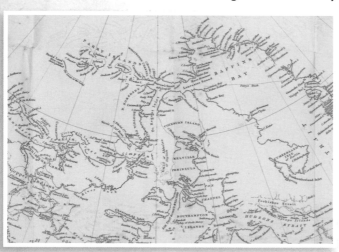

Map showing the limits of knowledge of the Arctic in 1846, from John Barrow's *Voyages of Discovery and Research within the Arctic Regions, from the Year 1818 to the Present Time.* Barrow was known for the numerous errors in his maps.

You are unaware of this milestone, of course, especially because your unexpected speed has lessened your original sense of doom. So has the mildness of the weather. Despite the dire warnings of the Danish whalers at Disko Bay, the temperatures are among the highest recorded in the Arctic, and the ice is at its lowest levels.

You decide there might even be an opportunity, perhaps when the ship is anchored in calm water near shore in one of the straits, to experiment with the newly invented Halkett boat that the Royal Navy sent along with the expedition. Made of rubber, it is an inflatable dinghy that can hold three men. It is a curiosity to be sure, but at least it will amuse and entertain.

The Halkett boat was designed as an inflatable solution to the problem of carrying boats over challenging Arctic terrain. This illustration shows the first design, the "boat-cloak." When it was deflated, the hull of the boat could be worn as a cloak and the sail used as an umbrella. The larger model Franklin tested could be paddled by two men and, when deflated, serve as a waterproof ground sheet.

In late August you see the low horizon of Devon Island. Beyond that is Lancaster Sound, familiar waters on the east west route south of Devon Island. Progress is fast and days blur one into the other.

You truly are in the lands that the Greeks called the Arktos. These lands lie beneath the constellation of the same name, Arktos Megale — in Latin, Ursa Major, or as you know it, the Great Bear. You are one of the few men in history to have been just as far into the Arktos as into the lands in the south that the Greeks called the Antarktikos, now known as Antarctica.

Time passes. A few weeks later, you are not surprised to see that pack ice — the ice that drifts with wind and current — blocks entry into Barrow Strait at the western end of Lancaster Sound. Franklin had hoped for open water there, to head south to where the coastal mainland awaits. His optimism is high, however, and to your surprise, despite the lateness of the season, he instead orders both ships north, up a wide channel where the water is still temptingly open.

Your mission is to forge the link between the known areas west of the Atlantic and the known areas east of the Pacific north. Franklin believes that at some point both ships can find another channel to navigate west again.

Franklin is wrong.

Navigation at Sea

Among Captain Francis Crozier's responsibilities on this voyage into the relatively unknown waters of the Arctic, one of the most crucial was tracking the ship's location, not only to find their way but also so that existing charts could be expanded for those who followed.

To know his location, Crozier would have relied on the ship's master to calculate the ship's latitude (distance north or south of the equator) and longitude (distance east or west of an imaginary north–south line that connects both poles, called the prime meridian).

To determine latitude, he would have used a sextant to compare the height of the sun to the horizon. To figure out longitude, he would have used marine chronometers, timepieces invented some 50 years earlier that allowed him to compare the time at his current location to the time at the prime meridian.

To calculate the speed of his ship? By 1845, ships were using mechanical "logs" made of metal and rope to measure speed. These were based on the older "chip logs."

The original chip log was a piece of wood tied to the end of a rope line with knots tied in the line at equal intervals. Once an hour, a crew member would toss the chip log overboard. When it hit the water, another crew member would flip over a small sandglass that emptied in 30 seconds. The chip would stay in roughly the same place it landed in the water while the ship moved away from it. When the top of the sandglass reached empty, the first crew member would reel in the line, counting how many knots the ship had progressed in that time span. From there, it was a simple matter of knowing the distance between knots and estimating how many "knots per hour" the ship was traveling — hence the phrase.

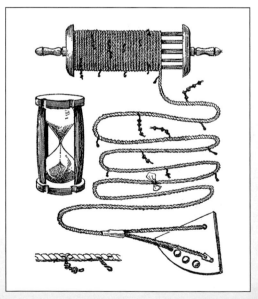

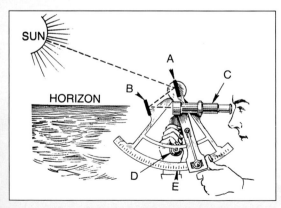

A sextant (above) and chip log (right) were early navigational tools.

(A knot measures speed, and a sea mile — or nautical mile — measures distance: 1 knot equals 1.15 sea miles per hour or 1.85 km/h.)

Equally important as location, especially in uncharted waters, was the depth of water. For this, Crozier would have depended on the oldest known piece of navigating equipment, used almost since the time that ships first took to sea — the lead line. It was a lightweight rope with "marks" made of fabric or leather tied on to it at regular intervals, and a weight attached to the end. The weight was made of lead, hollowed out at the bottom and filled with wax.

At one fathom — every 1.82 m (6 ft.) — there was a mark on the rope that a seaman would be able to see from a platform jutting out from the ship. The seaman would throw the lead line, wait for it to hit bottom and then call out the mark that was visible above the water's surface. ("Mark twain" meant exactly two fathoms.)

The depth wasn't the only crucial information given by the lead line. Particles stuck in the wax — like gravel or sand or mud — indicated what kind of bottom it had hit.

As it turned out, the first explorer to sail through the Northwest Passage — Roald Amundsen on the *Gjøa,* from 1903 to 1906 — did it with a crew of six and a much smaller ship. He had decided the only way it was possible was to live off the resources of the land and sea as they traveled, and for this to be possible, he needed to keep the crew as small as possible.

Amundsen's success, of course, proved that Sir John Ross had been correct some six decades earlier when he questioned the sizes of the *Erebus* and *Terror* and the amount of food that would be needed to sustain all the officers and crew of the Franklin expedition.

Roald Amundsen, Norwegian explorer, was first to sail the Northwest Passage.

The community of Gjoa Haven got its name from *Gjøa,* Amundsen's ship.

Eventually more ice blocks the ships, and you need to reverse course. Worse, the open water that brought you this far north is beginning to freeze, too. Now it is a race against the approach of winter. The drifting ice will continue to build, under such pressure that the force sometimes drives it as much as a half kilometer (a third of a mile) inland.

Because of your previous voyages in the Arctic, you understand too well the changing sounds of the ships' hulls in water.

First come the *glug-glug-glug* sounds of the ships' bows going through sludge ice. Sludge is a mush on the water's surface that is about as thick as honey.

Then at night, as you stand on deck huddled in your coat, you hear the *glug-glug-glug* sound change to rasping, like sandpaper against wood. This is the sound of pancake ice — slushy circular disks — the first sign of a freeze, but melting away each day.

You begin to worry when the pancake ice doesn't melt away but expands, joining together and building. It stretches from the shorelines out to your ships, 30 cm (1 ft.) thick, more than thick enough to walk on.

Now the race south again to Lancaster Sound is in earnest. Instead of retracing your route north through the Wellington Channel, between Cornwallis and Devon Islands, you travel south along the west side of Cornwallis Island.

The iron-plated bows of your ships can still push through pancake ice with little effort. Next, the ships must weave through multi-year ice, three times as thick as pancake ice. It builds up, filling in the gaps at the shorelines and creeping toward the center of the channel.

With the rasping sound comes the occasional thump — large slabs of drift ice banging into the hulls of your ships. And you know that growlers — large chunks of ice, still a far cry from iceberg size — are on the way.

The Crews of HMS Hecla & Griper *cutting into Winter Harbour, Sept. 26th 1819,* from Parry's *Journal of a Second Voyage for the Discovery of a North-West Passage.* Parry's crew cut through the ice to lead ships to harbor for the winter.

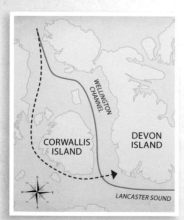

Ice forces a return south.

While you can steer around them, growlers are the same blue as the water around them and impossible to see early enough to avoid, as they rise only knee-high out of the water, with the bulk of the ice beneath. Growlers make a distinctive low sound as your ships push against them.

The Franklin expedition's Beechey Island winter quarters

You dread this growling sound because it's a warning of approaching hummocky floes — huge chunks of ice capped by snow — and now there are so many you can't count them all as the ice begins to trap both ships.

Your good fortune has turned. The best you can hope for is a place to anchor safely for the winter.

Franklin orders the ships to harbor just off Beechey Island, off the southwest corner of Devon Island. Here, monstrous rock cliffs on three sides give relative shelter from the howling winds that will come during an Arctic winter.

Bleak as this seems, you are not a stranger to a ship stuck in ice.

Anticipating the blizzards and gales that will pound those cliffs, you order all sails and ropes to be taken down. For the first time since leaving England, you are so busy that you don't have time to dwell on your heartache.

Parry's *Fury* and *Hecla* wintered at Igloolik in 1822–1823. Posts set in the ice mark a road to the land.

The uppermost masts are struck down as well, leaving still tall, but eerie stumps. You cover the decks with a foot of snow for insulation, then put sand on top to make footing easier. You order men to sink rows of posts in the ice to mark a road to the island. You order others to move provisions onshore to give more room in the cramped ships. You arrange for fire holes — squares almost 2 m by 2 m (6 ft. by 6 ft.) — to be cut into the ice for a steady supply of water in case of fire aboard ship.

It becomes a waiting game.

You will winter inside the ships. In the cramped lower deck, with only the stove to heat the interior, where Franklin hopes the library and other amusements will be enough to occupy officers and crew during endless hours of boredom.

For now, the crew build shelters onshore and exercise outdoors when possible. As days become weeks, your preparations for overwintering complete, you wait. You are about to be thrashed by blizzards and gales, with temperatures dropping below -50°C (-60°F). Without the coal aboard for heat, your ships would become icy tombs.

Your wait continues, day after monotonous day, through October and November and December.

Then the monotony ends on day one of the new year with the first death of one of your men.

Apply Forensic Techniques to
Solve the Mystery

At the time of his death, Ötzi was roughly 45 years of age. Found buried in ice high in the mountains along the Austrian-Italian border, he was carrying a primitive copper-bladed ax that could have come straight from a museum.

That, along with his clothing made of animal skin, was the first clue to how long he'd been dead — well over 5000 years. Using forensic techniques, scientists have been able to glean an amazing amount of information about the lifestyle of Ötzi "the Iceman," Europe's oldest known natural mummy.

High levels of copper and arsenic in hair strands suggest he might have been involved in copper smelting. The proportions of his leg bones are evidence of a lifestyle of climbing rugged terrain, as if he shepherded sheep in the mountains. He had internal parasites.

His teeth were filled with cavities.

Two other pieces of information also intrigue you, as a forensic scientist. Pollen found in his stomach show he'd eaten his last meal at a lower altitude. And X-rays and a CT scan show that he'd had an arrowhead in his shoulder, matching a small tear in his coat, which had been removed before death. Other DNA analysis shows blood from at least four other people — from one person on Ötzi's knife, two different people on a single arrowhead and someone else on his coat. And he was found frozen with his face down and left arm across his chest, with bruises and cuts to his hands, including a cut to a bone of his thumb that had not begun to heal.

What's your forensic conclusion about Ötzi's final hours?

Answer at end of the chapter.

THE SEARCH THEN : Warm Polar Waters

Sir John Barrow, October 1845: London, England

"As to the miserable thing called a map, which has been prefixed to Mr. Barrow's quarto … it is so defective that it can seldom be found of any use."

— William John Burchell, English explorer, naturalist, traveler, artist and author

Sir John Barrow had retired to enjoy London life and bask in his achievement, believing he'd fulfilled his life's ambition to bring England the glory of discovering the Northwest Passage.

Barrow was convinced that the North Pole was surrounded by the "Open Polar Sea," consisting of temperate and ice-free waters. He wasn't the only one, of course. In Barrow's lifetime, the Arctic North was one of the last unmapped areas of the globe. Theories abounded about what lay beyond the rim of ice that circled the top of the world. The world's foremost expert on maps, August Heinrich Petermann, was convinced that warm currents swirled around an island at the North Pole. The only obstacle for explorers was to make it through the belt of ice-pack waters south of the open waters. Then it would be plain sailing across the top of the world. Barrow wanted England's flag planted on that imagined island, just as much as he wanted England to claim the prize of finding a way across the top of the world.

Sir John Barrow, civil servant, geographer and writer

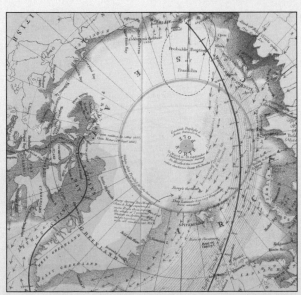

Petermann's maps of the Arctic showed the North Pole as an icy island surrounded by warmer waters.

There was some foundation for questioning Barrow's map skills, certainly when he was young. Some 50 years before the *Erebus* and *Terror* vanished over the Arctic horizon, as a young man yet to be granted a knighthood or given the title of baron, the highly ambitious Barrow had served as a private secretary in South Africa. He had a habit of taking copious notes and making sketches of the countryside, and at the end of his journeys published the first map of Cape Good Hope.

By all accounts, it was riddled with errors and, for all practical purposes, useless.

Years later, when his ambition and drive brought him to the powerful post of Permanent Secretary to the Admiralty, a position he held for decades, Barrow's confidence in his knowledge of maps gave him the optimism to organize another attempt, despite his earlier failed expeditions.

In 1817, reports reached Barrow that 46 620 sq. km (18 000 sq. mi.) of ice had disappeared between northern Norway and Greenland. That was all he needed as incentive to send two Royal Navy expeditions to the North the following spring.

The first of the two didn't even reach the east coast of Greenland before turning back, its ship *Dorethea* leaking badly after encounters with ice. Second-in-command of the expedition? Lieutenant John Franklin, who by the fall of 1845

After being stranded for four winters in the Arctic, and presumed dead, Captain John Ross and crew of the *Victory* were rescued in 1833 by the *Isabella*, the same ship Ross commanded in 1818. This hand-colored engraving is by Edward Francis Finden.

was somewhere back in those same conditions, this time with more expensive ships and higher expectations.

As for the other 1818 expedition, it departed for Baffin Bay, west of Greenland. Impenetrable ice pack blocked the top of the bay, and the commander lost all hope of finding a route to the so-called Open Polar Sea from there. That commander was Sir John Ross, who would try again in 1829 on a privately financed ship, *Victory*.

Barrow well knew how heroic the 1829 expedition had been.

Victory had been abandoned in Victoria Harbour on the east side of the Boothia Peninsula until finally destroyed by pack ice in 1832. After another winter, Ross had no choice but to lead his men on foot to a place of rescue, adding to his years of experience in Arctic conditions.

So as the officers and crew of *Erebus* and *Terror* began their first dreadful winter stuck in the pack ice, Barrow, who hadn't even seen an iceberg on his only trip to the North, would have had the luxury of raising a snifter glass of fine brandy, dreaming that both ships had already reached warm open waters near the North Pole.

Elsewhere at the time ...

The Aerial Wheel

Aerial wheel

While ships were the glamorous form of transport, carriages dominated the cobblestones on the streets of London, which made for a bumpy ride since the spoked wheels were clad with iron rims. What if there was another way?

This was the year that inventor Robert William Thomson applied for a patent to bring comfort to passengers in carriages and riders of bicycles. He'd already designed a method to set off charges of explosives via electricity. His newest patent led to something that would explode as well.

But not by design.

He called it the "Aerial Wheel." His invention used a thick leather outer skin to encase a rubberized fabric tube filled with air. Attached to the rim of the wheel, the tubular cushion of air made for a much smoother ride. Until, of course, it exploded. So, in a way, Thomson also invented the first flat tire.

OF SHIPS AND MEN : Black All Over

Louie Kamookak,
February 1982: Gjoa Haven, King William Island

Along the shoreline of Gjoa Haven, September 2019

The tiny community of Gjoa Haven (Ursuqtuuq) overlooks Arctic waters at the southeastern corner of King William Island. Since childhood, Louie Kamookak had lived through winters where the temperature regularly dropped to -40° and below. It is a killing cold for the unprepared. Skin exposed to the wind stings, then becomes numb, then burns from frostbite until the skin is dead and there is no sensation.

Through the elders' tales, Kamookak knew that the winters the Franklin expedition's officers and crew faced from 1846 to 1848 were far worse than winters in modern times — so severe that they had become part of Inuit legend.

He also knew that Inuit had decided the *qaplunaaq* — the white men — were to blame for unleashing evil spirits on the island during those horrible cold years. If so, they paid the price. Although Franklin's officers and crew had winter clothing and fur blankets, they lived through those winters without the luxury of down-filled coats, insulated boots or thick mittens. Without the clothing of animal hides that Inuit had adapted for extreme cold — layered in two parkas, the inner one with the fur against the skin, the outer with fur facing the wind. Without waterproof sealskin boots.

Kamookak heard about the severity of those winters directly from the elders he interviewed through the years. He also studied Charles Hall's written records from his journey to the area in the 1860s.

Hall, an American explorer, could not speak the language of the Inuit. However, he traveled with two Inuit interpreters who had learned to speak English from whalers and during time spent in England. In Arctic expeditions, Hall heard, and recorded, stories about cannibalism and sunken ships. One Inuk spoke of a boat with places on its sides that held air. It sounded a lot like the portable inflatable boat that Franklin had brought north.

Some Inuit told of four small boats hanging from a big boat, and a plank coming down from the boat to the ice. They had seen smoke coming from a chimney and were sure "some white men must have lived through the winter." Others later found the boat abandoned and locked up tight. There had been tracks — four men and a dog. A man named Aglukkaq.

In a separate story, an elderly Inuk from the Igloolik settlement spoke to Hall about Sir William Parry's ships stuck in the ice in the early 1820s. She mentioned the man they called Aglukkaq — Francis Crozier on one of his earlier expeditions — and how he had promised to return one day.

Most compelling was the witness of the Inuit woman who passed along the story to Hall of men with black faces, black hands and black clothes.

At that time, the Royal Navy was not prepared to give any credibility to Inuit stories. In London, Hall's two interpreters had been invited merely as curiosities for people to view. The Inuit stories delivered by Hall contradicted the heroic myth that the Royal Navy wanted preserved about the officers and crew. The official story was that the ice had trapped them and all had valiantly tried to escape the Arctic by marching out.

More than a century later in Gjoa Haven, Louie Kamookak, of course, had an entirely different perspective on the stories recorded by Hall. Kamookak began to compare stories for accuracy. He knew that because many of the details were so specific, there was no chance they had been fabricated.

"His [Louie Kamookak's] research has provided incredibly valuable insight that will help contribute greatly to this search."

— John Baird, environment minister of Canada in 2008

Ipirvik (Ebierbing), an Inuit guide and explorer who helped Charles Hall and, almost a decade later, Frederick Schwatka

Louie Kamookak sharing traditional knowledge with Gjoa Haven youth taking part in the 2015 Malerualik Expedition

Kamookak's first advantage as a modern searcher was his residence in Gjoa Haven. For anyone else to explore the island, it took hours of travel by air to reach it. Anyone else would face a harsh and dangerous landscape that for Kamookak had been part of his life since he was a boy, learning the land as he maintained traplines for foxes.

Most of all, Kamookak's greatest advantage was that he was Inuk.

He knew, for example, that in the nineteenth century, Inuit described direction by wind and position of the sun. To them, north was where the wind blew from, which on a magnetic compass reads as northeast. Likewise, to Inuit, south was where the southeast wind came from. For non-Inuit historians and explorers over the past century, that made for a lot of confusion in any search based on Inuit stories, because they based north and south on what their compasses told them.

By crisscrossing the territory of his people, Kamookak drew up a massive list of local names to construct family maps, which allowed him to map out traditional hunting grounds. In turn, that allowed him to specifically place some of the events described.

Beechey Island's protected harbor in summer

Black faces, black hands and black clothes? This wasn't a metaphorical way to describe the men of the ship. Kamookak was no forensic scientist, but he understood that men living in tight quarters and burning coal in a desperate attempt to stay warm during a polar winter would have clothing covered in black soot. Black faces and hands sounded like frostbite.

As for the big tent? Well, as Kamookak would learn, it hid a horrible secret. Human bodies stripped of meat. But we haven't got to that part of the story yet.

Kamookak was also intrigued by a map sketch drawn up decades earlier for Hall by an Inuk whose name Hall recorded as In-nook-poo-zhee-jook. (A modern Inuktitut spelling would be Inukpuhigruk.) The Inuk spoke of two ships — one that sank while the crew was trying to take goods off it, and another abandoned. He also said Inuit had found the courage to sneak onto the abandoned ship and found the body of a very large white man. This ship, he said, sank the next summer in water so shallow that the masts remained in sight.

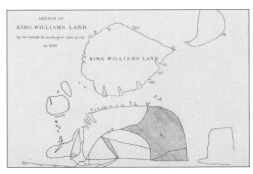

Sketch map of King William Land provided by In-nook-poo-zhee-jook to Charles Francis Hall, 1869

The Inuit evidence recorded by Hall was valued by everyone connected with the search for the wrecks. Surely, Kamookak believed, the more stories he heard and the more clues he uncovered, the closer he would get to helping solve the mystery of whatever happened to the Franklin expedition.

Inuit sharing and comparing maps with John Ross. From his *Narrative of a Second Voyage*.

Mystery SOLVED

Congratulations if you concluded that Ötzi the Iceman had been in a fight of some kind, one that probably began at a lower altitude, where he'd last eaten, and then continued as a chase going up into the mountains, where he finally fell.

The cuts and bruises suggest an ongoing fight. The blood on the arrowhead suggests that he hit two people with it. The evidence that he'd been able to retrieve it both times suggests he had killed those two people. The blood on his coat? That, you decide, could have come from a wounded comrade that he helped carry up the hill.

But ultimately, Ötzi lost the fight, taking an arrow in his shoulder. His facedown position and bent arm suggest that he had turned onto his stomach in an effort to pull the arrowhead loose, then died from loss of blood. This shows, once again, that the dead *do* tell tales.

EPISODE FOUR
Endless Night

BEECHEY
ISLAND

LANCASTER SOUND

BAFFIN
ISLAND

TIMELINE

MAY 1845: THE DOCKS AT GREENHITHE, THAMES RIVER, LONDON, ENGLAND

JULY 1845: DISKO BAY, GREENLAND

AUGUST TO SEPTEMBER 1845: LANCASTER SOUND

SEPTEMBER 1845 TO AUGUST 1846: BEECHEY ISLAND

AUGUST TO SEPTEMBER 1846: PEEL SOUND AND FRANKLIN STRAIT

SEPTEMBER 1846: KING WILLIAM ISLAND

SEPTEMBER 1846 TO JUNE 1847: LAT 70°05' N, LONG 98°23' W

JUNE 1847 TO APRIL 1848: SHIPS LOCKED IN ICE

AUGUST 1848: BOOTH POINT, KING WILLIAM ISLAND

SEPTEMBER 1848: MONTREAL ISLAND, MOUTH OF THE BACK RIVER

HUDSON
BAY

NORTH
AMERICA

CANADA

PACIFIC
OCEAN

UNITED STATES

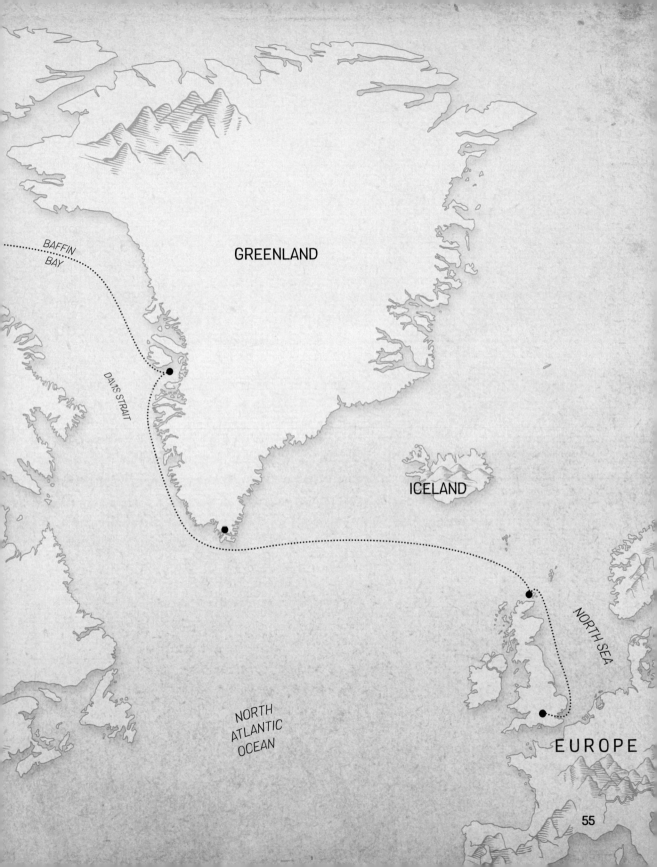

BAFFIN BAY

GREENLAND

DAVIS STRAIT

ICELAND

NORTH SEA

NORTH ATLANTIC OCEAN

EUROPE

YOUR EXPEDITION : First Death

September 1845 to August 1846:
Beechey Island

DEVON ISLAND

BEECHEY ISLAND

"The winter of the arctic regions had now come on us, in its character of gale, cold and snow …"

— Commander Robert McClure, searching for *Erebus* and *Terror* in 1850

Rats have long plagued sailing ships.

The darkness outside the ship is constant. The 24-hour night has settled on the frigid Arctic. At your writing desk, your oil lamp flickers whenever even the slightest draft of the howling blizzard outside seeps through the cracks of the closed hatch, one you cheerily had open during summer.

The Royal Navy requires you to keep a meticulous ship's log to record daily entries. You can flip back your pages and read routine entries like this:

August 15, 1845 5:30 AM Lashed up hammocks. 6:30 AM went to breakfast and every thing ready for starting but the weather proving unfavourable. The party were delayed. Carpenters caulking upper deck.

Briefly, you reflect on how much circumstances have changed since you smoothly sailed across Baffin Bay in August of the year before. Then you dip your pen into ink. When you lift it, you pause at the rasping sound of claws on wood. Idle curiosity lifts your eyes to track the sound. You know it will be a rat, boldly crossing the floor almost at your feet. The only question, really, is the size.

This one is large, gleaming black, its back bowed as it scuttles from one side of your cabin to the other. It pauses, looks back at you and then with a disdainful flick of an oily tail disappears behind a wash stand.

There is little point in pursuing it. Rats have gnawed holes in the paneling and this one has a dozen escape routes, the same routes it will use to return while you are sleeping. If you did manage to kill it, another would replace it before you flung its body into the fire of the stove.

You dip your pen to paper to record that the man who died, John Torrington, was only 20, and had been suffering from consumption, an infectious disease that had damaged his lungs. He was the lead stoker on your *Terror*. In the poorly ventilated hold of the ship, shoveling the coal into stoves to provide life-saving heat for all on board was a death sentence for him. The coal dust filled his already weak lungs to the point where he could hardly draw a breath.

You were aware of his existing illness, and while this first death saddens you, it does not alarm you — a sentiment that you add to the record in the ship's log. You record that Torrington was buried ashore on Beechey Island by lamplight and you settle back in your chair, staring at nothing.

Despite attempts to occupy and amuse the crew, you find it a miserable life in a world reduced to the belowdecks of the ships, something you dreaded when you accepted your post as second-in-command of the expedition.

From the deck hatch above, a ladder leads to this lower deck, the only portion of the ship to be heated. Officers have their own compact berths, while crew hang their hammocks 36 cm (14 in.) apart in the mess area, sleeping over the tables and chests where they eat. There is just over 2 m (7 ft.) of headroom in that long, narrow space, only about 9 steps wide, shared by 60 men. What light there is mostly comes from smoky lanterns.

The galley stove in the center glows with precious heat. The stove is also used to melt fresh snow and ice to provide necessary drinking water for all the officers and crew.

Your officer's quarters are so tiny that you can stretch your arms and touch all sides with your fingers. Still, you are more fortunate than the enlisted men, for you have a private place to sleep. Even then, you can't escape the coughing and sneezing and snoring and burping and flatulence and cursing of five dozen men who share the lower deck with you.

Illustration from *The White Slaves of England*, 1853. Coal mining was dangerous work. After a critical 1842 report, the government banned women and girls and boys younger than 10 from working underground.

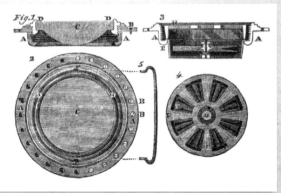

Preston's Patent Illuminator. These glass prisms were installed on the decks of the *Terror* and *Erebus* to let light in below during daylight hours.

These sounds, however, are welcome in comparison to the threats delivered by the unrelenting Arctic winter. Sleep comes fitfully. In the unheated deck below, at -50°C (-60°F), bolts and fastenings of the *Terror* freeze to the point of cracking, and shatter with the boom of pistol shots. Winds vary from constant moaning to howls that rock the ship. Ice scratches at the hull like skeleton fingers trying to dig through the

The Icebergs, by Frederic Edwin Church

wood. The pack ice itself roars as it buckles and breaks, sometimes with a force that makes it sound like someone has shot a cannon.

You and your men are not alone in this winter hell. You are surrounded by hundreds upon hundreds of those rats, who also seek the heat to survive. They scurry under the beds, up the walls, under the stove, in the lockers. You lift a cushion and a rat will burst away. You can hear them gnawing to keep their teeth sharp, so efficient they can bore through barrels and planking. They leave behind countless droppings. When you finally fall into fitful sleep, they bite you, waking you again and adding to your exhaustion. They pass along disease.

And they compete for food.

While you begin the journey with enough provisions for five years, the rats will multiply and gorge themselves on your food. Along with roaches and weevils. Assisted by mold and fungus and mildew. On a long voyage, this might destroy half of the food stores. Any commander expects this loss and plans for it.

But now, thanks to modern technology, much of your food is stored in cans, safe from rats and roaches and weevils and the mold and fungus and mildew.

Magnetic North Pole

One of Francis Crozier's previous expeditions to the North was considered a double failure. From 1824 to 1825, he and James Clark Ross served under William Parry in a search for the magnetic north pole. Not only were they unable to find it, pack ice destroyed one of the two ships in the expedition.

A few years later, Ross served under his uncle, Sir John Ross, on another expedition where, once again, pack ice claimed another ship. This time, however, James Clark Ross made an overland trip and on June 1, 1831, became the first European to reach the magnetic north pole.

That meant he was also the first European to be in a position for the needle of his dip circle to point straight down.

A dip circle and a compass both work because they consist of a small magnetic needle that can move freely within a casing. Like the Earth, magnets have two poles, north and south. In a compass, the north pole of the magnet is attracted to the south pole of the planet, and vice versa.

The Earth itself is a giant magnet of sorts. Its magnetic field starts in the interior, where, as a result of the Earth's rotation and because of heat escaping to the surface, molten iron in the Earth's outer core slowly swirls like lava. This movement generates electric currents that in turn produce the magnetic forces that reach from the core into outer space.

Anywhere on the planet's surface, the end of one compass needle will point to the magnetic north pole (not the geographical North Pole, which is some 1600 km or 1000 mi. to the north). At the magnetic north pole itself, the dip circle needle will be drawn straight down, as this is the only place on the planet where you are standing directly above it.

If James Clark Ross returned to that location today, however, he would no longer be at the magnetic north pole. At a rate of about 57 km (35 mi.) per year, the location of the pole shifts according to the shifting magnetic currents in the molten iron below.

In the past century alone, the magnetic north pole has moved 1000 km (620 mi.). That shift, however, is minuscule compared to something called geomagnetic reversal.

Yes.

Geomagnetic reversal is when the north and south poles flip entirely, something that's happened 183 times over the last 83 million years. The latest flip was a mere 780 000 years ago. Soon enough — at some random point in an unpredictable pattern — there is going to come a time when your compass won't point you to the north, but to the south.

GEOGRAPHIC NORTH POLE

MAGNETIC NORTH POLE

2010
2000
1950
1831
1850

While you accept that life inside an icy ship is something to be endured, your mind turns to the life you have left behind. You find yourself miserable thinking of the woman you love, the woman who does not return your affections. You do your best to settle back into routine after the Beechey Island burial of John Torrington.

Frozen graves of John Torrington, John Hartnell and William Braine on Beechey Island. Engraving by James Hamilton, based on a sketch by Elisha Kent Kane.

Three days later comes the second death, jolting you out of that monotony again.

This time — unlike when consumption struck — there is no warning. It happens on the *Erebus* to 25-year-old John Hartnell, who seemed healthy. Whatever killed him did it quickly.

This is so alarming that Franklin decides a crude autopsy is necessary. The *Erebus* surgeons cut open Hartnell's body and dissect his throat and heart and lungs. This shows some early damage of consumption as well, but consumption is a slow-moving disease and does not explain why Hartnell died within 72 hours of showing illness.

Hartnell, too, is buried on Beechey Island.

You count out more monotonous days belowdecks, enduring the winter, enduring your heartache. You pray there will be no more deaths. But your prayers are not answered.

Before spring arrives, and before the ships are set free from ice, comes the third death — Private William Braine — during a sledging expedition away from the ships. His body is dragged back, but this time the surgeons don't perform an autopsy, for his mouth is full of blisters, a symptom of scurvy.

Three deaths in such a short span is truly perplexing. This is an unusually high mortality rate for an expedition. After all, you spent four years exploring the southernmost parts of the Antarctic with your friend James Clark Ross. Four years, and you lost only a handful of men the entire time.

Three dead now, barely months into the expedition. Consumption — although infectious — should not have killed Hartnell, and scurvy should not have killed Braine. And even with those as causes of death, neither should have died so quickly.

It is your first indication that a killer is stalking your men. Later, you will discover the same killer will destroy the rats aboard the *Terror*. Right now, however, all you know as spring approaches is that something is already going horribly wrong.

Your premonition of doom returns.

Apply Forensic Techniques to
Solve the Mystery

He once took a long needle and inserted it between his eyeball and skull to see if his vision would change when he distorted his eyeball by pushing the needle against it. He also invented a new type of mathematics — calculus — and kept it a secret for 27 years. It was said that he was so easily distracted that on some days he would sit on his bed and think for hours, forgetting about plans he had made for the day.

And this was before he entered a time of his life that historians acknowledge was an extended bout of madness.

Despite these eccentricities, Sir Isaac Newton was an acknowledged genius. He formulated theories and mathematical equations that made sense of all the motions of the universe. He was the first to build a practical reflecting telescope, and he developed theories about the nature of light and color, using a prism to first show how light combined the colors of the rainbow.

His rational scientific mind, however, began to turn to mystic pursuits, including prophecies in the Bible. He was convinced he could find a way to turn lead into gold and spent hours alone in a lab in pursuit of this, tasting, smelling

Sir Issac Newton

and ingesting heavy metals. His full mental breakdown hit him in 1693, when he was 51 years old. He barely slept; he had paranoid thoughts about his friends and lashed out violently at those close to him. His symptoms also included chronic indigestion and depression.

As a forensic scientist, you have a theory about what caused his year of madness, especially after you study his notes about his methods in the laboratory. What forensic assumption led you to analyze strands of his hair, centuries after he died?

Answer at end of the chapter.

THE SEARCH THEN : First Warnings

Sir John Ross,
September 1846: London, England

Sir John Ross, born in 1777, was not a young man when he offered to search for Franklin.

As the summer of 1846 passed, Sir John Ross, nearing 70 years of age, was expected to retire from the Royal Navy. Still no word had come from Franklin. Short of reaching the Pacific, Franklin's only method of communicating their progress was to drop canisters into the ocean waters.

The Admiralty seemed unworried by the expedition's continued silence. After predicting easy success, it would be politically inconvenient to admit that anything might have gone wrong.

Not so for Ross, who had been studying the previous 40 years of weather records of northern cities such as Copenhagen and Stockholm, Arkhangelsk and St. Petersburg.

Ross concluded that extreme cold in northern Europe indicated the same weather for the eastern Arctic. He predicted — with no way of knowing how correct he was — that Franklin wouldn't even be able to make it much past Cornwallis Island before the first winter.

Ross's fears grew in the summer of 1846. Whaling captains were reporting that the eastern Arctic was experiencing unusually severe cold weather and the sea ice was far thicker and more extensive than in previous years.

Because of the failure of his 1829 expedition, Ross remembered too well the horrible toll inflicted on officers and crew by each successive winter stuck on the ice. Time was a devastating opponent in the Arctic, when ice packs could crush ships at whim and sailors had no way of hunting for fresh food.

This was crucial to Ross because he didn't trust the canned provisions. In the months after provisioning the *Erebus* and *Terror*, Stephan Goldner had also provided canned goods for more expeditions. However, Royal Navy seamen on other ships had been complaining about finding the guts of animals and non-meat items, like pieces of bone, in Goldner's tins, which were often bent out of shape and released horrible-smelling gases when they were opened.

Ross made the correct assumption that if the *Erebus* and *Terror* were going to find and complete the Northwest Passage, they would have succeeded by the end of the second summer of the expedition. He had no doubt that they would have been able to communicate this success after reaching the Pacific.

He believed they were trapped, and he couldn't wait any longer to get permission to search for them.

On September 28, 1846, Ross wrote his first letter to the Admiralty: *Having promised to Sir John Franklin, that, in the event of the expedition under his command being frozen in (as the one I directed was for four years) I would volunteer in the year 1847 to proceed to certain positions we had agreed upon in search of him and his brave companions …*

His offer was refused. One of the reasons given was the Admiralty's steadfast confidence that Goldner's canned provisions would keep the officers and crew not only alive but in good health no matter how many winters in pack ice it took for the *Erebus* and *Terror* to make it through the passage.

Sir John Ross asked the Admiralty for permission to search for Franklin.

Elsewhere at the time …

Letheon

We know it as ether — a pleasant-smelling colorless liquid that can be vaporized into a gas that puts people to sleep. While John Ross was sounding the alarm about the *Erebus* and *Terror*, on the other side of the Atlantic, in Boston, Dr. William Morton applied ether to a patient and performed the first painless tooth extraction. Shortly after, another Boston surgeon removed a tumor from the neck of his patient using the same technique.

Morton wanted to cash in on this and tried to pass off ether as "Letheon" so that he could apply for a patent. The benefits to the medical community were plain to see. Not only did unconscious patients not suffer pain, but surgeons could operate at a slow pace without worry that the patient would move.

Happily, it was soon discovered that Morton's Letheon was simply ether, and across the world, knocking out patients with ether became standard operating procedure.

OF SHIPS AND MEN : First Autopsy

Owen Beattie,
August 1984: Beechey Island

Beechey Island is not much more than a gravel beach — just a spit of land and freezing wind — off the southwest coast of the largest uninhabited island in the world, Devon Island. On the eastern slope, sheltered by large cliffs from nearby land masses, the headboards of the graves of John Torrington, John Hartnell and William Braine, the first three sailors to die on the expedition, are the most prominent features of a bleak landscape.

Here is where the expedition had wintered from 1845 to 1846, in relative safety from winds provided by the cliffs on each side. The sailors' graves, the first physical indication of the ships' route through the Arctic, had been discovered by searchers in 1850. Since then, the bodies had been undisturbed. Could forensic science help solve the mystery of the Franklin expedition?

Three years after his time on King William Island, Canadian scientist Dr. Owen Beattie was back in the Arctic, searching for more answers.

The bones his team had discovered in 1981 on King William Island had already revealed one clue to the fate of the officers

The original gravesite headboards at Beechey were black with white carved inscriptions. The wood weathered white over the years. In 1976, the headboards were sent to the Prince of Wales Northern Heritage Centre in Yellowknife for preservation and replaced with replicas with bronze plaques.

and crew. It was a gruesome story, one that had already been told by Inuit, although for a long time denied by the Royal Navy.

Yet there was another surprise from those bones, something that only forensics could reveal.

In the months that followed his return from King William Island, Beattie tested the bones for trace elements to learn more about the diets of the officers and crew. What he learned was something of incredible significance to anyone trying to solve the mystery of what had happened to the officers and crew.

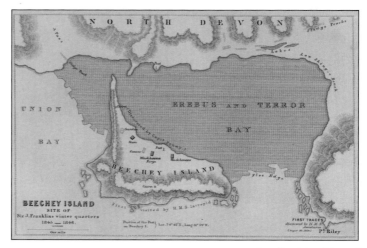

Beechey Island Site of Sir J. Franklin's Winter Quarters 1845–1846, map by A. Petermann, 1852. *Erebus* and *Terror* wintered in the bay east of Beechey Island, later named Erebus and Terror Bay by searchers.

Results showed that skeletons found nearby of Inuit individuals from the same period had lead levels from 22 to 36 parts per million (ppm), typical of the bones of humans from cultures that have no exposure to lead. Bone that was believed to be from a crewman of the expedition showed, at a minimum, levels of 228 ppm, enough to cause lead poisoning.

Lead poisoning.

This could explain what appeared to be erratic behavior by the crew and men. Earlier searchers had found smaller boats full of heavy but useless items from the ship. They could not understand why the men had bothered to drag these heavily loaded boats. Why, indeed, was one of the boats pointed northward, when the march across the ice was supposed to have been in a southward direction?

While symptoms of lead poisoning include fatigue and weakness, abominable pain, tingling in hands and feet, headaches and constipation, it's the human brain that is most sensitive to lead. Lead poisoning causes confused thinking and behavioral problems.

Yet this finding only drew Beattie to another mystery. Where had the lead come from? Food tins? Lead-wicked candles? Pewter?

As a forensic scientist, Beattie knew that high levels of lead in the bones of the sailors might simply be the result of a gradual buildup, a lifetime of exposure to lead. He needed a forensic examination of soft tissues to see if the lead exposure had occurred only during the voyage. That soft tissue, he hoped, would be found on the bodies on Beechey Island.

In August 1984, with permits to open the graves, Owen Beattie and his team had only a short window of time. The month of May is too cold, and July too warm, filling the low marshy sands with meltwater.

John Torrington

They started with John Torrington's grave. It took two days of chipping through permafrost before a strange smell reached Beattie and his team. Until then, they didn't even know if they would find a body, since sometimes dummy graves were made for sailors who had died by falling overboard.

When they were finally able to pull back the fabric that covered Torrington's face, they saw it was so well preserved by the permafrost that encased it that it seemed as if the sailor had died only a few days earlier. They soon realized his body showed signs of starvation.

The second grave held two major surprises. The first was that someone had previously exhumed John Hartnell's body.

The second? It had already been autopsied.

The first mystery was solved by the contents of an unpublished letter from the leader of an 1852 private expedition to the island. Commander Edward A. Inglefield, sent by Lady Franklin, wrote to the Admiralty a description of opening the coffin and then restoring it in place as carefully as possible.

As for discovering the Y-shaped cut of a medical autopsy in the torso? The conclusion was that surgeons of the expedition had done this before burying Hartnell. That told Beattie — and was fresh information to historians — that nearly a century and a half earlier, the second death of a sailor had already alarmed the expedition leaders.

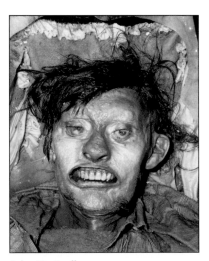

John Hartnell

As for William Braine, in the third grave, his body was in the worst condition, showing signs that rats had gnawed at his body before burial.

Beattie and his team collected hair and other soft tissues for later analysis. Away from the graves, they examined discarded tins, tins that showed sloppy soldering with globs of lead on the inside of them. Scientists who believed the ships had still been heated by hot water pipes lined with lead thought those pipes were also a cause of contamination. Later researchers said a different system, installed for the Franklin expedition to melt snow and ice for drinking and bathing, would have produced lead-contaminated water.

Although the forensic evidence eventually revealed that the three men had died of a combination of pneumonia and tuberculosis (called consumption at that time), if the hair and tissue samples that Beattie took back to his laboratory showed high lead content, those cans and lead pipes could be a major contributor to their deaths.

And yes. Analysis showed vastly elevated levels of recent lead ingestion. It appeared that a major cause of the expedition's disaster had been lead poisoning.

For the next 30 years, this conclusion would be accepted as truth.

Discarded tins on Beechey Island

 # Mystery SOLVED

Congratulations if you concluded that Newton's symptoms pointed toward mercury poisoning, resulting from the fumes in his laboratory and his habit of ingesting heavy metals. One of his hairs showed 197 ppm of this toxic metal, compared to the normal level of 5.1 ppm.

While some historians point out there is some difficulty in knowing the authenticity of the hair you tested (was it really Newton's?), your conclusion seems to fit the facts. Especially because you know that the effects of mercury poisoning are reversible, and the later parts of Newton's life, when he was no longer experimenting, showed much more sanity.

Newton: 197 ppm

Normal: 5.1 ppm

EPISODE FIVE

Fateful Decisions

BEECHEY ISLAND

LANCASTER SOUND

PEEL SOUND

FRANKLIN STRAIT

BAFFIN ISLAND

HUDSON BAY

NORTH AMERICA

CANADA

PACIFIC OCEAN

UNITED STATES

TIMELINE

MAY 1845: THE DOCKS AT GREENHITHE, THAMES RIVER, LONDON, ENGLAND

JULY 1845: DISKO BAY, GREENLAND

AUGUST TO SEPTEMBER 1845: LANCASTER SOUND

SEPTEMBER 1845 TO AUGUST 1846: BEECHEY ISLAND

AUGUST TO SEPTEMBER 1846: PEEL SOUND AND FRANKLIN STRAIT

SEPTEMBER 1846: KING WILLIAM ISLAND

SEPTEMBER 1846 TO JUNE 1847: LAT 70°05' N, LONG 98°23' W

JUNE 1847 TO APRIL 1848: SHIPS LOCKED IN ICE

AUGUST 1848: BOOTH POINT, KING WILLIAM ISLAND

SEPTEMBER 1848: MONTREAL ISLAND, MOUTH OF THE BACK RIVER

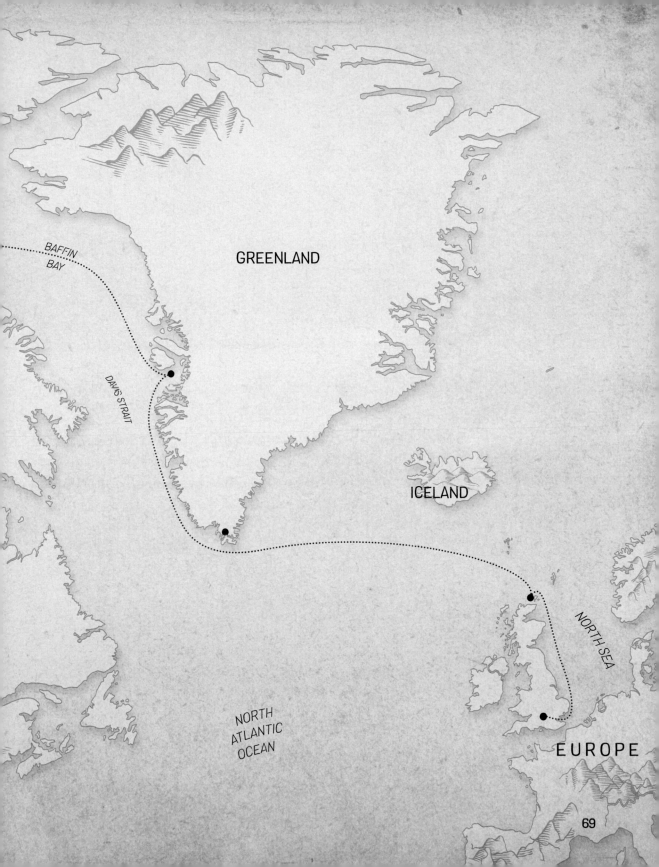

BAFFIN
BAY

DAVIS STRAIT

GREENLAND

ICELAND

NORTH SEA

NORTH
ATLANTIC
OCEAN

EUROPE

PRINCE
OF WALES
ISLAND

SOMERSET
ISLAND

PEEL SOUND

FRANKLIN STRAIT

BOOTHIA
PENINSULA

YOUR EXPEDITION : Failed Gamble

August to September 1846:
Peel Sound and Franklin Strait

"No vessel could have gone south through Peel Sound. All I could see for fifty miles was an unbroken sheet of ice."

— Explorer James Clark Ross, reporting on his unsuccessful 1848 search for *Erebus* and *Terror*

The smallest cracks of daylight — at first lasting only minutes each dawn — begin to lengthen dramatically each week, until the 24-hour darkness becomes 24 hours of daylight. The ice finally releases *Erebus* and *Terror* from the bay off Beechey Island.

As your ship cuts through the water, your spirits rise. It is summer. The western portion of Lancaster Sound is open. It was no sure thing. Steady Arctic winds can pile ice up in one location or the other, just as easily as it pushes froth across the surface of the frigid waters.

To your surprise and delight, you discover a channel that makes a line straight south. In September, it had been filled with ice and looked no different than the islands on each side. Now, amazingly, it is a promising doorway of glittering blue, dotted with small bobbing ice floes.

Behind you is the last headland marked on your charts. You are now in waters that haven't been explored.

HMS *Terror* anchored near a cathedral-like iceberg in waters around Baffin Island, 1836. Painting by Sir George Back, Arctic explorer.

It would have been prudent to stop occasionally and send men to shore to leave behind messages for those who might follow you. It would have been equally prudent to unload some provisions and leave them behind as caches in case anything goes wrong and you need to retrace your route.

But the weather is too good. Your progress too easy. You wonder if Franklin is too confident. And the summer season too short. You have 400 km (250 mi.) of channel that goes straight south. Straight south! Surely you will reach the mainland soon, and all that remains is to follow the coastline west to the Pacific Ocean and triumph.

Day after day, you stand on the deck of the *Terror*. On the one hand, the poetically spectacular scenery buoys your heart. After the bleak white landscape of a polar winter, color flashes every direction you look. The greens and teals of the water, the purples and blues of blossoms on bushes of the treeless islands on each side, the reds and lavenders of light reflected off ice floes. The water itself is alive with the activities of seals and walruses and whales. Truly, summer in the Arctic is a joy.

You give no consideration to shooting the seals and the walruses from the ships' decks. It would waste bullets and powder and leave behind floating carcasses. To bring the ships to a complete halt is a gargantuan task, and by the time you did, those carcasses would be long out of sight. To anchor and send crew out in rowboats to hunt would squander days of easy sailing, when you know the window of time of relatively ice-free water will last only a matter of weeks. Besides, you have plenty of canned provisions. Starvation is the remotest of possibilities.

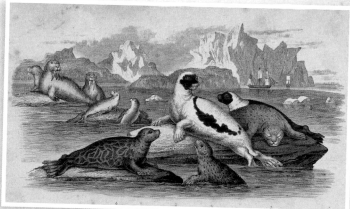

Eight different specimen of seals sitting on ice floes in the Arctic sea. Colored etching by J. Bower after J. Stewart.

Yet such an open landscape makes the ships — large as they are — seem insignificant, and you fight a feeling of depression, for it reminds you of the solitude of your soul. Humans are built for companionship and, time and again, you become melancholy thinking of your loneliness. If not Franklin's niece, then who? And what is worldwide fame without someone to share it with?

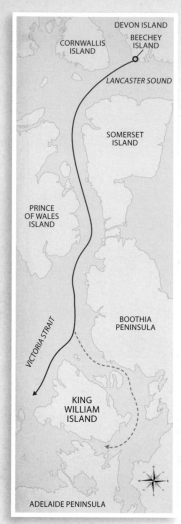

The ships travel the shorter, western route through Victoria Strait, marked here in red, rather than head east around King William Island. Is this route a deliberate choice or do prevailing conditions force it? No one knows.

High above you in the mastheads, lookouts keep a keen eye out for pack ice that might be jammed into the channel by wind. Finally, they spot King William Island.

Finally! You are certain of your location.

You know this because of previous Arctic explorations. In 1824, you were part of William Parry's disastrous Arctic expedition with James Clark Ross. In 1829, James Clark Ross joined his uncle, Sir John Ross, in another attempt to find the Northwest Passage. With ships stuck in ice, their expedition was forced to make an overland trek, on foot, and charted the area, which they called King William Land. Although you have not seen this for yourself, John Rae will later report that the land was actually an island.

This is how you now know that it will be only a short trip to the southern end to reach the mainland. West from there, maybe 400 km (250 mi.), you will reach the open waters that will make you victorious in completing the Northwest Passage. At your rate of progress, this may take less than a month.

Ever a pessimist, you can't believe it will be this simple.

But Franklin is jubilant. At worst, if the ships don't make it all the way to the Pacific before winter, they will be in position to do so the following summer.

There is a decision to be made, however. Head east around the top of King William Island to go down the eastern side? Or choose what looks like a shorter route, down the western side, the channel named Victoria Strait? The drift of the ice pack seems to make it logical to go down Victoria Strait.

Days later, too soon — and too late to turn back to try the eastern route — comes the dreaded *glug-glug-glug* of sludge ice. You strain your eyes as you peer ahead with the telescope for signs of any further obstacles that will block your progress.

The sounds from the ships' hulls follow a predictable pattern. *Glug-glug-glug* becomes the rasping of pancake ice, followed by drift ice, then the ominous growlers that warn of hummocky floes.

Climate Change in the North and the Northwest Passage

MV *Nunavik*

In July 2019 — at that time, the hottest month ever measured on the planet — record temperatures in Greenland meant that the ice sheet on the island, the world's largest, was melting at the unfathomable rate of 11.3 billion metric tons (12.5 billion tons) per day. (Melted, that much would cover the entire state of New York with 25 cm, or 10 in., of water.)

This is as good an indication as any of how climate change is affecting the Arctic. That month, essentially no ice existed in Lancaster Sound, where at the end of the summer 174 years earlier, it would have been blocked by ice.

Indeed, according to one oceanographer, the Arctic is currently experiencing the fastest warming on Earth.

On King William Island — where the *Terror* and *Erebus* were stuck offshore in pack ice for a winter, then summer and winter again — it is now so warm that grizzly bears from the south have appeared and even mated with polar bears, producing hybrid prizzly bears, or grolar bears, depending on your choice of words. The island is now home to dozens of species of birds that have never before been north of the Hudson Bay lowlands.

A grolar bear

What was once inconceivable is now becoming a reality: commercial cargo and cruise ships crossing the Northwest Passage unimpeded by ice.

In 2014, this happened for the first time. Unescorted by icebreakers, the MV *Nunavik*, a cargo ship loaded with nickel bound for China, departed Canada's Deception Bay on September 19 and reached Point Barrow in Alaska only 11 days later. The 40 percent fuel savings that come from shaving such great distances off the journey are a tremendous incentive for other cargo ships to do the same. The total time for the MV *Nunavik* to reach China was 26 days. The traditional route before the building of the Panama Canal, down to the tip of South America and up the Pacific, would have taken 41 days.

It's predicted that within a generation, the route through the Northwest Passage will be available year-round. Ironically, if that does happen, it will help fight one of the factors most scientists argue have contributed to our warming planet. By taking this shortcut, the MV *Nunavik* reduced its greenhouse gas emissions by about 1300 metric tons (1430 tons).

Taking a Sextant Reading Near the Beset Terror, on Valentine's Day, 1837. From George Back, *Narrative of an Expedition in H.M.S.* Terror.

Lookouts above confirm: ice pack ahead to the south and the west.

You are about to learn that the constant Arctic wind has pushed hundreds of thousands of tons of ice into the channel where it has no outlet to escape. If you could have chosen the longer, eastern way around King William Island, would you have succeeded in reaching the mainland? You will never know, and it doesn't change your situation.

You argue to Franklin that here, where the summers are short, it is nearly the end of summer. Yes, there are still long weeks before winter truly hits, but this far north of the Arctic Circle, the weather can turn savagely cold at any time. In the waters ahead, one week or one day too long can be the difference between escape or being pinched into an ice pack that can crush a ship.

You argue that it would be best to use this window of time to find a safe spot to anchor and wait until next season to reach the Pacific.

Franklin faces a difficult decision. Despite your best preparations, an unprecedented three men died during the previous winter. Franklin cares deeply about his men and doesn't want to have to lead any more graveside services. Large open veins of water in the ice pack tempt him to gamble. The crew members, too, are anxious to keep going. After all, the ships are in excellent shape and, with the right conditions and open water, they could reach their goal in a matter of days.

You point out that if you are not anchored in time, trapped ships will literally sit atop a shifting mountain of ice. Perched like that, the *Terror* and *Erebus* would be at the mercy of a relentless flow of ice, ice that would grind the ships for all of the months of blizzards and gales, and nearly a year of savagely low temperatures.

You argue you need to find safe haven near land, just as you did the winter before, off Beechey Island.

But you are only second-in-command. Despite the knowledge and experience you bring to the arguments as the single man who has spent the most voyages in Arctic and Antarctic winters, Franklin has the final say.

Franklin commands the ships to steam ahead into the ice-choked waters. The crew is unaware of the dangers that you described to Franklin. While they cheer his decision, your premonition of doom grows stronger than ever.

Your fear is justified, but not only for the reasons you argued to Franklin.

What you don't know is that burning coal in a useless fight to advance westward will unleash the killer that lurks in the holds of the *Terror* and *Erebus*.

Apply Forensic Techniques to
Solve the Mystery

Whetstone from Baffin Island

On Ellesmere Island, the most northerly Arctic island, Inuit archaeological sites dating from around 1200 CE contain evidence of contact with the Norse who occupied Greenland at the time. Iron nails, fragments of chain mail and a portion of a bronze balance of the type used by Norse merchants to weigh coins indicate contact and probably trade between Norse and Inuit.

Inuit tradition tells us that when their ancestors first moved to Arctic Canada, the Inuit found it already occupied by a people whom they called Tuniit. The Tuniit seem to have disappeared shortly after the Inuit arrived, and it is commonly held that they vanished before any contact with Europeans.

Yet on Baffin Island, the fifth-largest island in the world, straddling the Arctic Circle, archaeologists found a site where Tuniit artifacts are present together with items resembling those of medieval European technology, including whetstones for sharpening metal blades.

Were the Tuniit in contact with the Norse who arrived in Greenland about 1000 CE?

As a forensic scientist you realize that you will need unmistakable evidence of European technology. How do you proceed from here?

Answer at end of the chapter.

THE SEARCH THEN : Foxes as Messengers

Sir John Richardson, July 1848: Mackenzie River

Three years earlier, in 1845, Sir John Richardson had opened an envelope and unfolded Franklin's letter. At that time, he had no inkling they would be the last words he'd ever receive from his friend and companion explorer.

Nor would Richardson have foreseen that he might take another overland trip into the Arctic some 20 years after the Coppermine expedition, where Franklin had to eat shoe leather to stay alive.

This time — even though the august members of the Royal Navy's Admiralty publicly maintained there was no reason for alarm — his mission was not to map coastline but to search for any evidence that Franklin and the officers and crew might still be alive.

While Admiralty members had been able to ignore the early alarm

The Arctic Council plans a search for Sir John Franklin (left to right): George Back, William Parry, Edward Bird, James Clark Ross, Francis Beaufort, John Barrow Jr., Edward Sabine, William Hamilton, John Richardson, Frederick Beechey. Painting by Stephen Pearce.

calls from Sir John Ross, they were unable to resist mounting pressure from members of Parliament, newspapers and Lady Franklin.

Because of that, the Admiralty decided to send out three different search parties to find Franklin, the *Erebus* and *Terror* and their officers and crew.

James Clark Ross, John Ross's nephew and a close friend of both Franklin and Crozier, was given two ships —

HMS *Enterprise* and HMS *Investigator* — to try to retrace Franklin's route into the eastern Arctic. It was not an easy decision for him. He'd retired and promised his wife he would never go to sea again. Yet if his actions could save Crozier's life … he saw no choice.

Another ship, HMS *Plover*, was sent the long way — south via the Atlantic Ocean, around the southernmost tip of South America and back up the Pacific Ocean to the Bering Strait of Alaska to begin a search of the western Arctic.

As for Sir John Richardson? He was to join John Rae, an experienced Arctic explorer, in smaller boats on an inland trip to Great Slave Lake and from there to the Mackenzie River, the longest in North America, which flowed into the Arctic Ocean. They were to reach the northern coastline and continue the search.

All three of these, the first of dozens of expedition searches, ended in failure.

James Clark Ross's search to retrace the expedition and find his close friend Crozier? Ice defeated the ships long before they could get far into the passage from the eastern side. As they wintered, Ross was so desperate to try something that he and his men trapped live foxes to use as messengers. Yes, as messengers. Each fox was fitted with a copper collar that gave details about the location of Ross's relief expedition. Ross released those foxes on the slim chance that any survivors lost somewhere in those those vast expanses of snow and ice might discover one of them.

The trip up the western side of South and North America to head eastward along the known portions of coastline from the Pacific? The *Plover* was a slow ship and did not reach Alaska for a year and a half, only to conduct an equally unsuccessful search.

Richardson and Rae? Two years of harsh travel produced no clues to the fate of the expedition.

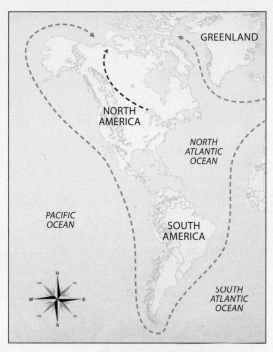

Three early rescue attempts: Ross (green) got stuck at Somerset Island. HMS *Plover* (blue) sailed around the continent to search from Alaska. Richardson and Rae (red) traveled inland and up.

Arctic Fox, from Ross's *Narrative of a Second Voyage in Search of a North-West Passage*

In 1848, James Clark Ross set out with the *Enterprise* and *Investigator* in search of the Franklin expedition.

During all of this, however, Stephan Goldner, purveyor of canned goods, profited more and more. He was the one to supply all the ships — *Plover, Enterprise* and *Investigator* — for the search for the Franklin expedition. These and future relief expeditions became his main source of income.

The disappearance of the *Erebus* and *Terror* was making him a rich man.

Elsewhere at the time ...

The Bankrupt Sawmill That Led to a Boost in the National Economy

Sir John Richardson's trek through the Arctic would have kept him from knowing that he would return to discover a world enthralled by a story about a mechanic and carpenter named James Marshall, whose discovery in California shaped the future of the next decade in the United States.

When Marshall and partner John Sutter decided to build a water-operated sawmill, he found some shiny stones in the streambed. After pounding the stones with larger rocks and discovering how easily they flattened, Marshall announced he had discovered gold.

As a consequence, more than 300 000 people flooded California, raising the population enough for it to reach statehood. At the same time, all that gold boosted the American economy.

The reward for James Marshall and John Sutter? Their sawmill failed because, thanks to the California Gold Rush they'd kicked off, they couldn't find able-bodied men to work for them, and hordes of prospectors forced them off their land. Neither ever did profit from the find.

Panning for gold during the California Gold Rush

OF SHIPS AND MEN :
A Line of Skeletons
David Woodman,
May 2002: Skull Island

Near what he would call Skull Island, David Woodman methodically drove a snowmobile along a 20 km (12 mi.) search path. He would finish that line, then turn and make a parallel line, pulling a sled made from wood that carried a magnetometer, with a rope long enough to keep the snowmobile from affecting its readings. The magnetometer was an instrument used to look for tiny magnetic fluctuations to help locate underground pipelines.

Woodman, however, was on ice above water, listening for any pinging sounds to indicate the wreckage of the *Erebus* or *Terror*. This wasn't his first search for one of the ships of the lost expedition. If he could find it, it would prove that he — like Louie Kamookak — had been right to take the time and effort to understand how clues found in Inuit oral tradition could make sense of a note found at Victory Point at the northern

David Woodman, explorer and author of *Unravelling the Franklin Mystery: Inuit Testimony*

tip of King William Island, a note of 138 words describing the fate of the ships and how the men had departed on foot to the south.

Indeed, in 1992 and 1993, field work on the western shores of King William Island provided crucial confirmation. Led by Franklin scholars Barry Ranford and Mike Yarascavitch, archaeologists and forensic anthropologists found nearly 400 bones and bone fragments of the crew, as well as artifacts such as buttons, brass fittings and clay pipes.

Frederick Schwatka interviewed many Inuit and had great respect for their knowledge.

The findings of these, the NgLj-2 excavations, seemed to confirm the Royal Navy's narrative of a brutal heroic march and a permanent abandonment of the ships.

Woodman, however, wondered if there was more to the storyline, in particular the location of the *Erebus* accepted by most historians. He himself was a navy person, serving as a second officer and navigator on a Canadian oceanographic research ship. His experience on the northern seas gave him a sense that Inuit were correct. It led him to write a book he felt Franklin experts would view as idiocy, so he let the manuscript sit on a shelf at his home for two years. Then his wife decided she would send it to a publisher. To his surprise, not only was his *Unravelling the Franklin Mystery: Inuit Testimony* published, but the experts began to use it in their own research.

Kamookak's focus was on listening to elders for clues about the expedition's fate. Woodman sifted through the records of Charles Francis Hall from his expedition in the 1860s, and cross-referenced them with another expedition from 1878 to 1880 led by another American, Lieutenant Frederick Gustavus Schwatka, who had been sponsored by the American Geographical Society.

The note left by Crozier and Fitzjames spoke of abandoned ships. Woodman became convinced that sailors had returned to those ships, and that Inuit went on board and spoke with the sailors.

He was further persuaded by what he read in Schwatka's accounts: the American had discovered a grave at Victory Point that held the body of a crewman identified as Lieutenant John Irving of the *Terror*. Irving had been mentioned as alive in the 138-word message of April 1848. His properly dug grave was proof that he'd returned to Victory Point sometime after the message was written. This matched Inuit accounts that they had met men on the northwest corner of King William Island *after* the officers and crew had first departed.

A line of skeletons marks the southward journey of Franklin's crew. These were men so weak they simply died as they walked. With Irving's grave as evidence, Woodman believed that at some point the departing party had divided into two, with some returning to the ships.

After hours of sifting through Inuit stories, Woodman also believed some of the men had still been alive a full four winters after the ships had been abandoned.

Finding either ship would be epic, almost like finding the Holy Grail. The Victory Point note told the story only to April of 1848, where all that was known for certain was the location of the abandoned ships stuck in ice. Yet nothing in the note contradicted Inuit evidence that suggested the ships did not sink there but, once released from ice, drifted to a fate in an entirely different location. If he could find a ship in this area, far to the south of where the 138-word note said they had been abandoned, there was the tantalizing possibility that objects or bodies in the ship would shed more light on the mystery. If only that ship could be located. And what if the ship's logs of the journey were found?

For Woodman, that was enough motivation to endure the difficulties of negotiating pack ice and dealing with magnetometer batteries that lasted no longer than two and a half hours in the severe cold.

Over two seasons, from 2002 to 2004, Woodman's team dragged the magnetometer over 310 sq. km (120 sq mi.) of ocean floor.

And found nothing.

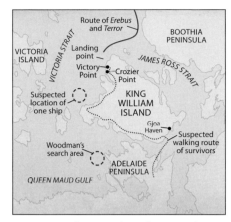

This map, based on Woodman's map, shows where the ships were believed abandoned and possible wreck locations. Note the area labeled "Woodman's search area."

Schwatka's search party identified a grave and skeleton at Victory Point as Lieutenant Irving's because of an engraved medallion found nearby.

Mystery SOLVED

Congratulations if you decided to look for other evidence to support your theory.

Using a technique known as energy dispersive spectroscopy, you examine wear grooves on the whetstones found. You detect microscopic streaks of bronze, brass and smelted iron — all pointing to a European presence.

This allows you to draw an exciting conclusion: the Arctic world of trade between Vikings and Inuit was probably more complex than anyone has realized to this point.

EPISODE SIX

No Retreat

TIMELINE

MAY 1845: THE DOCKS AT GREENHITHE, THAMES RIVER, LONDON, ENGLAND

JULY 1845: DISKO BAY, GREENLAND

AUGUST TO SEPTEMBER 1845: LANCASTER SOUND

SEPTEMBER 1845 TO AUGUST 1846: BEECHEY ISLAND

AUGUST TO SEPTEMBER 1846: PEEL SOUND AND FRANKLIN STRAIT

SEPTEMBER 1846: KING WILLIAM ISLAND

SEPTEMBER 1846 TO JUNE 1847: LAT 70°05' N, LONG 98°23' W

JUNE 1847 TO APRIL 1848: SHIPS LOCKED IN ICE

AUGUST 1848: BOOTH POINT, KING WILLIAM ISLAND

SEPTEMBER 1848: MONTREAL ISLAND, MOUTH OF THE BACK RIVER

PEEL SOUND

LANCASTER SOUND

FRANKLIN STRAIT

BAFFIN ISLAND

KING WILLIAM ISLAND

HUDSON BAY

NORTH AMERICA

CANADA

PACIFIC OCEAN

UNITED STATES

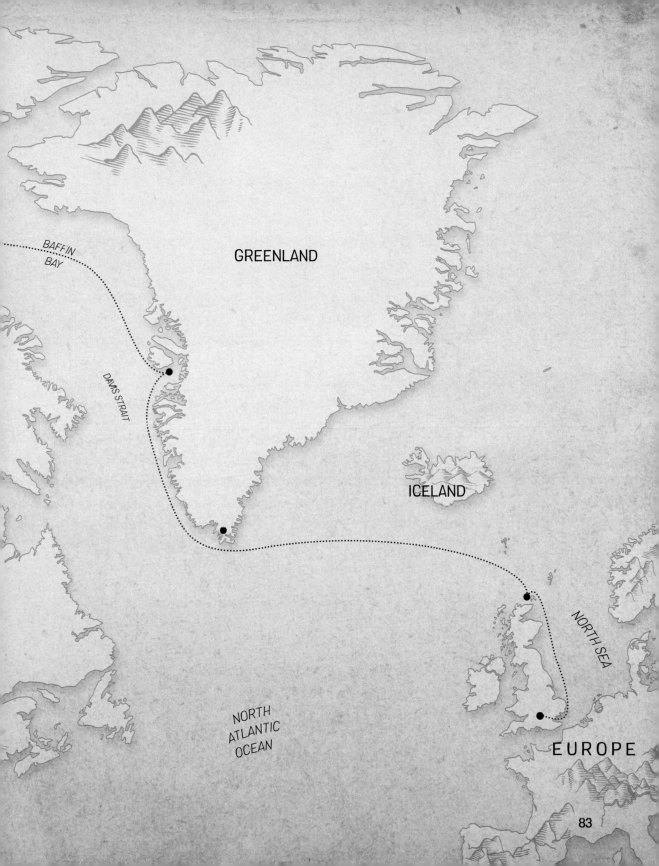

BAFFIN
BAY

GREENLAND

DAVIS STRAIT

ICELAND

NORTH SEA

NORTH
ATLANTIC
OCEAN

EUROPE

PRINCE
OF WALES
ISLAND

BOOTHIA
PENINSULA

KING
WILLIAM
ISLAND

YOUR EXPEDITION : Ice Closing In

September 1846: King William Island

You stand, legs spread apart to keep your balance, on the deck of the *Terror* as it lurches back and forth. Thick sooty smoke from the exhaust of the ship's steam engine mushrooms upward in a column through the frigid air. The slap of waves against the hull has been replaced by the huffing of the engine as stokers belowdecks shovel coal into the white glow of the boiler's firebox. The smoke fumes are dark and oily, and you wonder if the engine will explode from the strain.

It is early September. Temperatures have plunged and what was loose ice has become as thick as wet cement. You take no satisfaction from knowing that Franklin should have heeded your advice and prepared the ships for winter by seeking safe anchorage.

Instead, you worry about how little coal remains. When it first became apparent that ice was closing in, Franklin doubled down on his gamble and pushed ahead, hoping to find open water on the other side of the ice.

The *Erebus*, with a larger steam engine, leads the way to try to push through the ice. Temperatures drop even more. Ice thickens. At full steam, burning through the coal reserves, the ships barely manage a walking pace.

Your estimate is that, at best, you have less than 14 full days of coal to power the steam engines. Your bigger concern is having enough coal to heat the ships during the upcoming winter. Without coal, the certainty is that all of you will die.

Lieutenant John Irving's drawing of the *Terror*'s adapted steam locomotive engine

You have an ironic thought. Sir Barrow had predicted the steam engine would set your ships free. Instead, it has led you into this trap. As a result, the prize is no longer winning a race for the Northwest Passage. Again, it's winning a race against a polar winter.

You have few options. Continue to gamble that you will break free of the pack ice to open water and then continue to burn coal at an incredible rate? Or conserve your coal and turn back immediately, hoping it's not too late to get out of the ice pack and find the type of safe anchorage that helped you survive the previous winter off Beechey Island? After heating the ships all winter, that might leave you enough coal for one final effort through the Northwest Passage when winter ends. Or so you hope.

HMS Erebus *in the Ice, 1846,* by Francois Etienne Musin. The icebergs and other details of this painting are not especially realistic.

You have another thought that you don't dare share. The best thing to do at this point? Abandon one ship and load all its coal and provisions onto the other. You wonder if Franklin, with his eyes on conquering the ice, would find this unthinkable. You keep this advice to yourself.

Within barely a day, when it becomes apparent that the ships have no chance of moving forward, Franklin finally makes the safe decision to retreat. But it's too late. Ice closes in so rapidly that not even the most modern technology in the world — horsepower delivered by steam engines — is able to conquer it.

Yet the lives of all, officers and crew, depend on escaping from the ice. How can you quit?

How Icebreakers Break Ice

Around the world, different countries have designed icebreaker ships in different ways.

The Chinese ship *Xue Long* is designed for the bow of the ship to cut through ice like a knife. As a smaller icebreaker, it is capable of crunching down through 1 m (3.3 ft.) thick ice at a slow, steady pace.

The Swedish *Odin* has a square-shaped bow. It uses hydraulic pumps to lift the ship onto ice and then, like Odin's hammer of ancient folklore, smash through with up-and-down movements.

Most icebreakers, however, are designed like bathtubs, with rounded keels that slide forward, up and onto the ice and then use the weight of the ship to break through.

With this method, the Australian *Aurora Australis* can handle ice 1.2 m (4 ft.) thick and more by backing up and ramming forward again.

The American *Polar Star* is large enough to crunch through ice 1.8 m (6 ft.) thick while cruising at a leisurely 3 knots per hour. By backing up and ramming, it can cut through an incredible thickness of 6.4 m (21 ft.) of ice.

The largest icebreakers in the world — the Russian Arktika-class ships — can cruise through 2.7 m (9 ft.) of ice without stopping to back up and ram forward again. By 2025, Russian icebreakers being built now will be able to tackle ice 4.6 m (15 ft.) thick at continuous speed.

The purpose of these massive icebreakers is to create a channel behind them so that cargo ships can follow in their wake. The distance behind is determined by ice conditions. The current Arktika-class ships leave behind open water some 33.5 m (110 ft.) wide; future ships will create water highways 60 m (200 ft.) wide, enough for the world's largest cargo ships to trail behind.

The reason for building larger and larger icebreakers?

With the ice cap thinning because of global warming, the Russians are betting that their future icebreakers will finally be capable of making regular routes through the Northwest Passage a reality, even before climate change makes this possible for all cargo ships.

In retrospect, it seems remarkable how far Franklin's expedition, with wooden ships and 20-horsepower steam engines, managed travel in conditions far more challenging than today's.

Three modern icebreakers: *Yamal, Louis St-Laurent* and *Polar Sea*

You send teams onto the ice. Twenty-four hours a day, they use 3.6 m (12 ft.) ice saws, picks, axes, ice chisels and even gunpowder to blast the ice. Inside the ships, you move cargo back and forth, shifting weight to rock the ships up and down. You even send anchors out ahead to set in the ice and then pull on the chains to drag the ships toward the anchors.

Crews of the Isabella and Alexander *Sawing a Passage Through the Ice,* from John Ross's *A Voyage of Discovery,* 1819. The anchors were used to help haul the ships forward through the ice.

For a week, this works. The progress is excruciatingly difficult and even more excruciatingly slow. But the closer to shore the ships are anchored, the better the odds of surviving the winter.

On the night of September 14, however, the ice closes in completely and wins. The next morning, when you send lookouts high above onto the masts, you get back the grim news. The ships are stuck in a vast wasteland of ice in all directions as far as the eye can see.

You are 40 km (25 mi.) from the nearest land, the northern tip of King William Island. During all your previous expeditions, you have never seen ice this thick and this ferocious. And you are stuck in it, trapped in a moving glacier that will grow thicker and higher after the sun vanishes, at the start of a long polar night. You will face the grip of millions upon millions of tons of ice grinding like the tectonic plates of an earthquake fault line. The resulting pressure ridges, towering like cliffs and often building faster than a man can run, will violently attack your ships, pushing them upward and upward, tilting them in one direction and then another.

Decades later, in the Antarctic, Sir Ernest Shackleton's ship, the *Endurance,* would be trapped in a similar situation. It was tilted so violently that it almost flipped end over end, and as the decks broke, Shackleton and his crew of 28 had to abandon ship.

Here you are, with more than 120 men in two ships. Winter has yet to begin. You are unable to guess where the current beneath the ice will take you.

All you know for sure is that your ship is like a fleck of paint on an endless horizon painted blinding white, trapped in shifting pressure ridges that can crush a ship's hull as if it were only eggshells.

You doubt it can get worse.

You are wrong.

Apply Forensic Techniques to
Solve the Mystery

In 1972 in a rocky crevasse in Greenland, grouse hunters found a traditional burial site of six Thule Inuit adults and two Inuit children. The bodies were stacked one on top of the other, with animal hide between each body. Sub-zero temperatures and a location with drainage and protection from weather had essentially freeze-dried them all, turning them into accidental mummies. The skin, hair and eyebrows of these Inuit were so preserved that tattoos were still visible, and it was possible to examine internal organs, including contents of the intestines.

They are known as the Qilakitsoq mummies, named after the Inuit settlement where they were found, settled some 1000 years earlier but long since abandoned.

Of particular interest to you as a forensic scientist is that you discover soot in the lymph nodes of their lungs and moss and lice in their intestines.

What conclusions do you draw?

Answer at end of the chapter.

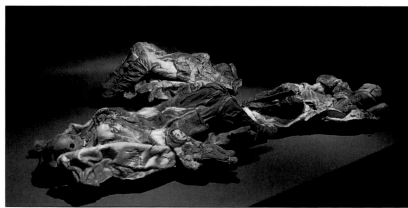

Qilakitsoq mummies

THE SEARCH THEN : Little Weesy

Lady Franklin,
August 1850: London, England

In Baffin's Bay where the whale fish blow
The fate of Franklin no man may know
The fate of Franklin no tongue can tell
Lord Franklin alone with his sailors do dwell

And now my burden it gives me pain
For my long-lost Franklin I would cross the main
Ten thousand pounds I would freely give
To know on earth, that my Franklin do live

— "Lady Franklin's Lament,"
popular English ballad

Lady Franklin, age 24, when she was Jane Griffin

Lady Franklin embroidered this sledge flag with Sir John Barrow's motto and sent it to the Arctic with a rescue party.

Among those in England obsessed with the mystery of where Franklin had disappeared, the most prominent was Lady Franklin, a woman even willing to communicate with the dead for help in finding her husband.

She was tireless in pursuing publicity to raise money and interest in the search. (Among those she contacted was U.S. President Zachary Taylor, who showed an interest in helping, but then promptly died of horribly severe diarrhea after eating too many cherries and raw vegetables at a July 4 celebration.)

Lady Franklin didn't stop at fundraising through letter writing and newspaper publicity. She also offered reward money from her modest family fortune.

As for communicating with the dead?

Lady Franklin visited clairvoyants to see if there were spirits on the other side who might be able to offer clues to the location of the *Erebus* and *Terror*. She gave close attention to one ghost in particular, belonging to a four-year-old girl, Louisa Coppin — Little Weesy, as she was called — who had died of typhoid fever.

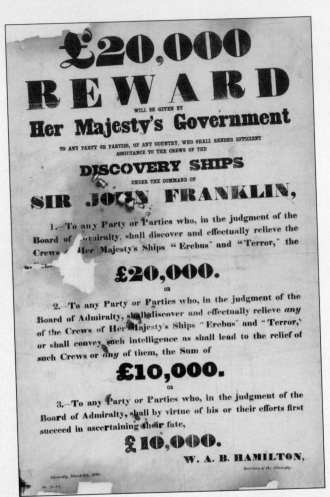

£20,000
REWARD
WILL BE GIVEN BY
Her Majesty's Government
TO ANY PARTY OR PARTIES, OF ANY COUNTRY, WHO SHALL RENDER EFFICIENT
ASSISTANCE TO THE CREWS OF THE
DISCOVERY SHIPS
UNDER THE COMMAND OF
SIR JOHN FRANKLIN,

1.—To any Party or Parties who, in the judgment of the Board of Admiralty, shall discover and effectually relieve the Crews of Her Majesty's Ships "Erebus" and "Terror," the

£20,000.

OR

2.—To any Party or Parties who, in the judgment of the Board of Admiralty, shall discover and effectually relieve *any* of the Crews of Her Majesty's Ships "Erebus" and "Terror," or shall convey such intelligence as shall lead to the relief of such Crews or *any* of them, the Sum of

£10,000.

OR

3.—To any Party or Parties who, in the judgment of the Board of Admiralty, shall by virtue of his or their efforts first succeed in ascertaining their fate,

£10,000.

W. A. B. HAMILTON,
Secretary of the Admiralty

Admiralty, March 8th, 1850.

A government reward poster offered £20 000 for "discovering and relieving" the crews; £10 000 for doing the same for any of the crew (or "conveying intelligence" leading to such relief); or £10 000 for "ascertaining their fate."

Louisa's father, Captain William Coppin, was a prominent shipbuilder. He visited Lady Franklin to report that the little girl's apparition was so real that when she appeared in the household, her brother would run to hug her, then bounce off a wall with such force he would inflict bruises on himself.

Coppin also told Lady Franklin that when Louisa's seven-year-old sister, Anne, once asked if Louisa knew anything about the expedition, Little Weesy's ghost disappeared, leaving Anne with a vision of the Arctic on the floor. Her vision showed two ships trapped in ice at the end of a channel. The seven-year-old girl then drew a map of what she remembered, which Coppin presented to Lady Franklin.

It's been suggested that Coppin already had a hunch about the ships' location and merely made up the story about a ghost so he could bring it to Lady Franklin. However, what is eerie in retrospect are three things. The accuracy of the chart the girl drew. The fact that the channel and island on the map were not discovered or put in any charts of the Arctic for another three years. And the more improbable accuracy of the locations of the ships when searchers were looking nowhere near those waters.

Yet efforts by Lady Franklin and Captain Coppin to get the Admiralty to search those locations were, no surprise, "but paper pellets on the hide of the rhinoceros." Lady Franklin might have been desperate enough to rely on directions from the dead, but the Admiralty wasn't interested in that kind of advice. They were determined to search with the solid assurance of ships and crew, although with just as little success.

As each expedition returned, reporting no signs of the *Erebus* and *Terror*, the mystery of their fate deepened.

One report, however, did lead to an important clue. A year earlier, the Admiralty had sent HMS *Plover* down around the tip of South America and back up the Pacific to the Bering Strait in an effort to explore the western Arctic for Franklin.

It was about this time that HMS *Herald* brought more than 4535 kg (10 000 lb.) of Stephan Goldner's preserved meats to HMS *Plover*. Little did they know that an Admiralty inspection would later find that meat in a "pulpy, decayed and putrid state and totally unfit for men's food." The remaining cans were dumped overboard.

HMS *Herald* and *Plover* meet in the Bering Strait in July 1849. Both were part of the search but neither found a trace of the Franklin expedition.

Elsewhere at the time ...

Obaysch into Prison, Convicts Out

Five years after the *Erebus* and *Terror* vanished from sight along the Thames, Lady Franklin was still an expert at drawing media attention. However, not even she could take the public stage away from a new visitor named Obaysch, who arrived in London by ship from Egypt.

A prison of sorts was waiting for Obaysch, where up to 10 000 people a day — a day! — crowded into the London Zoo for a glimpse of his thick body, short legs and massive snout. After all, Obaysch was the first hippopotamus to be seen in Great Britain since prehistoric times. No wonder the fate of the *Erebus* and *Terror*

Crowds look on in 1852 as Obaysch the hippopotamus rests behind bars in the London Zoo.

seemed a dull and distant memory to most.

At the same time, convicts by the hundreds were taken out of crowded British prisons and packed onto ships, to be sent across the world to populate another island, a continent actually, this one with animals just as strange to England as hippos: kangaroos.

OF SHIPS AND MEN :
A Different Kind of Poison

**Preserved in a Thumbnail,
2013 to 2016:** Two New Conclusions

*"Every growing tissue has a
story to tell."*

— Dr. Jennie Christensen

To searchers and historians like Louie Kamookak and David Woodman, it seemed more and more that the traditional Royal Navy narrative of a heroic death march in a final effort by the officers and crew to find rescue needed to be questioned.

In the same way, cutting-edge tools of forensic science began to suggest that the theory that lead poisoning was a major contributor to the deaths of the officers and crew of the *Erebus* and *Terror*, accepted as truth since 1986, was not entirely correct.

Beattie's analysis all those years earlier had shown that, indeed, lead levels were elevated in the soft tissue samples of the sailors. That indicated that the lead levels in bones were not only from long-term lifetime exposure but also

Grave of John Hartnell, HMS *Erebus*, on Beechey Island

potentially from the lead in canned food and in the water-piping system on the ships.

In 2012, to confirm this hypothesis, Dr. Ronald Martin, professor emeritus at Western University in London, Ontario, and his team used high-energy X-ray beams to examine vertebrae and tibia fragments from John Hartnell's burial site on Beechey Island and fragments found on King William Island.

Martin's analysis showed no difference between the lead levels concentrated in older and newer bone materials of the crew. If the crew had been poisoned, as supposed in Beattie's theory, there would have been a spike of levels in the newer bone samples.

Perhaps the long-accepted theory of lead poisoning wasn't accurate. Yet what would explain the spike in lead levels in soft tissues and hair that Beattie had discovered? That answer would need just a little more time.

After all, Beattie did not have some of the forensics tools available in 2016. But toxicologist Dr. Jennie Christensen did, with the advanced analysis techniques provided by laser ablation, the synchrotron particle accelerator and stable isotope analysis.

Laser ablation is a method of vaporizing tiny layers of a solid with laser beams.

A crude analogy for the synchrotron particle accelerator is to think of a circular tube, like a covered racetrack, but on a much smaller scale. Particles, not cars, are accelerated through an electromagnetic field in a vacuum, and variations in the guiding magnetic field can increase the relative masses of those particles.

As for stable isotope analysis, this is a method that compares the molecular weights of different elements.

Big words, complicated technology, but simple results. Shave off tiny flakes of something, run those flakes through the accelerator to get the sizes of the elements within those flakes, and do a comparison of the sizes to see which elements are present.

Toys and cribs used to be painted with lead-based paint, until it was discovered that even tiny bits of lead can cause severe poisoning, especially in teething children.

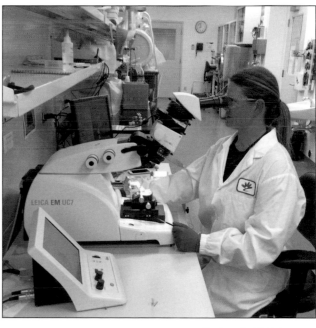

Dr. Jennie Christensen, toxicologist and environmental scientist, working at the lab

John Hartnell's coffin on Beechey Island

Forensic scientists can access this technology to see if drugs or poisons may have led to death. In 2020, for example, a woman was convicted of killing her husband by adding eye drops to his drinks, essentially poisoning him with tetrahydrozoline. This was determined by examining the deceased man's blood.

Dr. Christensen used these forensic tools to measure levels of copper, zinc and lead in a toenail and thumbnail from John Hartnell's body. Fingernails and toenails consist of alpha-keratin, which is essentially the tough protein also found in hair, horns and claws. As hair and nails grow, elements in the blood bind to the keratin and provide a permanent record of nutrients and toxic metals ingested during that growth.

Christensen and her team discovered that Hartnell had been severely zinc deficient. This would have suppressed his immune system. And this, in turn, allowed tuberculosis to attack, leading to his death.

As for the higher-than-expected lead levels? As Hartnell's body broke down because of illness, the lead stored in his bones was likely released into his bloodstream, which showed up in strands of his growing hair and nails.

The photos of the exhumation here, opposite and on page 66 are by Brian Spenceley, who joined Beattie's team for the research trip. Spenceley was a great-great-nephew of John Hartnell and his brother Thomas, both members of the expedition.

Interestingly, people affected by a zinc deficiency share similar symptoms of confusion as those who suffer from lead poisoning. Would this explain some of the strange behavior that Inuit observed in the sailors?

The lead poisoning theory had almost been dismantled.

Almost.

Arctic cold preserved John Hartnell's body so he looked almost lifelike when he was exhumed.

Mystery SOLVED

Congratulations if the forensic report gives you insight into the customs and lifestyle of the Thule Inuit all those centuries past.

The tattoos would have been made by drawing a needle through skin, with a thread-like sinew dipped into soot to serve as ink. The soot would have come from lamps that burned seal oil, soot that the Thule Inuit would also inadvertently inhale in the confines of small shelters.

The moss is equally easy to understand, showing that the Thule Inuit ate plants to offset a meat-heavy diet of fish, marine mammals and reindeer. But why would they add the lice found in their intestines to their diet?

You realize that this — like the inhaling of soot — was an accident. The mummies show that lice infested the bodies and the furs of the Thule so heavily that the lice became part of the food that they were eating.

Most of the female mummies from Qilakitsoq showed signs of facial tattooing. It is thought that they received tattoos at puberty and marriage, which would explain why a younger female did not have tattoos.

EPISODE SEVEN
Landfall

Lat 70°05' N,
Long 98°23' W

PEEL SOUND

FRANKLIN STRAIT

LANCASTER SOUND

BAFFIN ISLAND

KING WILLIAM ISLAND

TIMELINE

MAY 1845: THE DOCKS AT GREENHITHE, THAMES RIVER, LONDON, ENGLAND

JULY 1845: DISKO BAY, GREENLAND

AUGUST TO SEPTEMBER 1845: LANCASTER SOUND

SEPTEMBER 1845 TO AUGUST 1846: BEECHEY ISLAND

AUGUST TO SEPTEMBER 1846: PEEL SOUND AND FRANKLIN STRAIT

SEPTEMBER 1846: KING WILLIAM ISLAND

SEPTEMBER 1846 TO JUNE 1847: LAT 70°05' N, LONG 98°23' W

JUNE 1847 TO APRIL 1848: SHIPS LOCKED IN ICE

AUGUST 1848: BOOTH POINT, KING WILLIAM ISLAND

SEPTEMBER 1848: MONTREAL ISLAND, MOUTH OF THE BACK RIVER

HUDSON BAY

NORTH AMERICA

CANADA

PACIFIC OCEAN

UNITED STATES

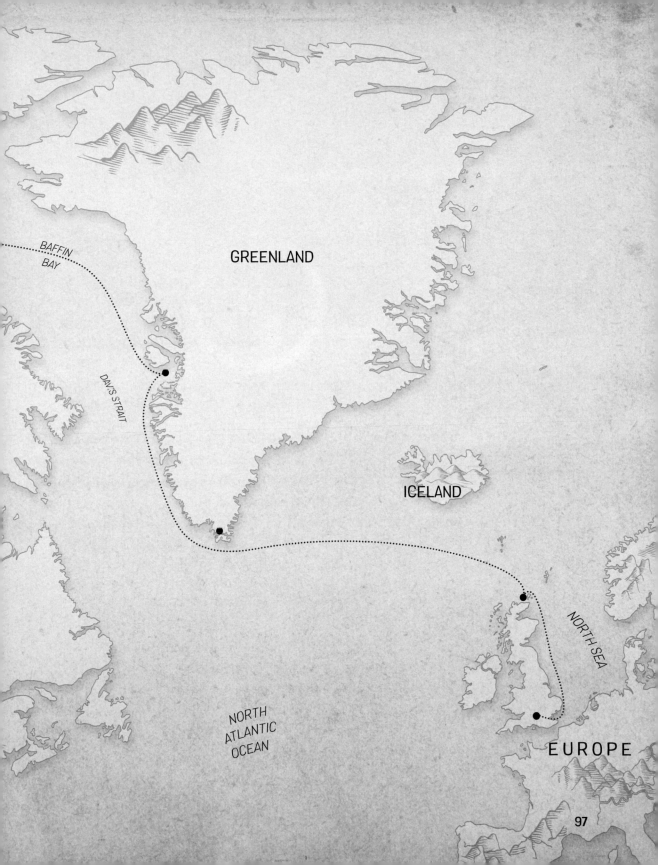

BAFFIN
BAY

GREENLAND

DAVIS STRAIT

ICELAND

NORTH SEA

NORTH
ATLANTIC
OCEAN

EUROPE

PRINCE
OF WALES
ISLAND

BOOTHIA
PENINSULA

Lat 70°05' N,
Long 98°23' W

KING
WILLIAM
ISLAND

YOUR EXPEDITION : All Well

September 1846 to June 1847:
Lat 70°05' N, Long 98°23' W

You wake each winter morning weighed down with the awareness that the pack ice is inexorably pushing your ships higher and higher on pressure ridges. And burdened by all of your responsibilities.

Belowdecks in the murky light of oil lamps, standing in front of you are able seaman William Jerry and the ship's assistant surgeon, Alexander McDonald. Your conversation is interrupted by cannon booms of exploding ice and the pistol shots of fastenings shattering in the -50°C (-60°F) temperatures. In the darkness of the perpetual Arctic night, you are literally adrift on a slow-moving mountain of constantly shifting layers of ice. Although you can lurch to keep your balance, you have no control over what fate lies ahead for your ships. Will the next pressure ridge snap your hulls? Flip the 300-ton ships like chips of wood in a river current?

Nor, it seems, do you have any control over the scurvy that is spreading from man to man. From your earlier expedition in the Arctic, you know that lemon juice loses effectiveness over time, becoming so weak in the fight against scurvy that portions from the 18 L (5 gal.) kegs of juice need to be doubled.

Even so, the scurvy gets worse.

William Jerry is 29 years old, with thinning reddish hair and a short, stocky body. He signed up from Pembroke, a village in the southeast corner of Wales.

Symptoms of scurvy included gums swelling, teeth falling out, painful skin lesions, swollen joints and lethargy.

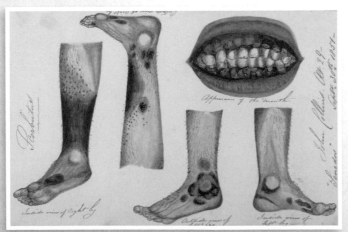

He expected to share in the fame and fortune that would come with defeating the Northwest Passage.

Instead, it is defeating him.

He opens his mouth for the assistant surgeon to inspect. You see that the gums of his mouth are spongy, bleeding and purple. It is no surprise to you. Jerry's bulging eyes were enough of an indication that he has fallen victim to scurvy. The only question is how advanced it has become.

He shows you his arms, which are mottled with bruises. His skin is scaly, dry and brown. On his shoulders is evidence of the dozens of strands of hair that have broken off at the scalp. The joints of his elbows are round and swollen. He grimaces with the pain that comes from movement.

Dr. James Lind experimented by feeding lemons to sailors sick with scurvy. From the collection of Michigan Medicine, University of Michigan, Gift of Pfizer, Inc., UMHS.17.

You let out a deep breath, feeling a sense of defeat yourself. Jerry is not the only one to have presented himself to the ships' surgeons. Scurvy moves slowly but with certainty.

In the library of 2900 volumes aboard both ships, three books offer only a little help: Dr. Lind's *Treatise of the Scurvy* and *An Essay on the Most Effectual Means of Preserving the Health of Seamen*, and *Observations on the Diseases of Seamen* by Sir Gilbert Blane. It doesn't take much to cure scurvy, just proper food. In the late 1700s, Dr. Lind had proven this, and since then, citrus fruits had literally saved hundreds of thousands of lives of sailors aboard ships with voyages longer than eight weeks.

With the kegs of lemon juice growing less and less effective, it appears there is no hope for your men. You watch in despair as scurvy takes hold and you know full well what lies ahead for William Jerry.

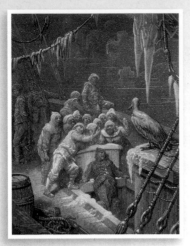

"I looked upon the rotting deck, And there the dead men lay." Scurvy features in *Moby Dick* and other seafaring tales popular in the 1800s, such as Coleridge's *Rime of the Ancient Mariner*.

His gums will grow over his teeth and then protrude so badly from the mouth that surgeons will need to trim the excess gums away. The pain in the joints will go from painful to unbearable. His arms and legs will begin to swell like sausages. The moist membranes of his nose will begin to bleed. Too soon, his blood vessels will rupture and blood will weep from the roots of his hair. Weakened, his body will be vulnerable to any one of a number of diseases that might kill him before scurvy takes away his willpower to move. Then death itself would be a mercy from the agony of the final stages of scurvy.

As the symptoms grow worse among your men, you fear that at least half of them will die. Half! You are too keenly aware of stories about Spanish galleons found floating with entire crews turned into corpses strewn about the decks.

Then, a miracle. Delivered by the new technology of food preserved in cans. Ironically, because the coal reserves are so low.

History of Scurvy

"A falling down of the whole soul" was how a seventeenth-century scurvy expert described it. He wasn't referring to all the horrible physical symptoms that made afflicted sailors smell disgusting to those around them.

Instead, it's a description of the extreme disappointment of a sailor waking from vivid dreams of food. The lack of vitamin C that led to scurvy also affected the brain, which would produce hallucinations. Sailors who craved food would see images in their sleep and face the emotional devastation of waking to discover it wasn't waiting for them to eat. Crew and officers were known to weep with this disappointment.

The beginning of the 1600s to the middle of the 1850s is often called the Age of Discovery because of global exploration by ships. It's also when scurvy killed an estimated two million sailors who contracted it after living weeks at sea without fresh fruit and vegetables.

In 1747, a Scottish doctor for the Royal Navy, James Lind, conducted one of the first ever clinical trials and developed a theory that citrus fruits and juices would cure scurvy. Despite Lind proving this, it took until 1794 for the practice to become common — so common that British sailors eventually became known as Limeys, from, of course, the limes they consumed.

To save fuel, the weekly issue of salt meat is reduced. It takes too much fuel to melt fresh water to soak and fry the meat. Bread, too, is reduced because flour needs baking.

To maintain the coal reserves, the decision is made to begin to deplete the reserves of canned food, which does not consume the precious coal needed for cooking or baking. Your men are given canned meat, canned vegetables and canned soup.

Erebus and *Terror* in pack ice, rocked by gale conditions

Within days, the scurvy symptoms begin to recede. These foods, your surgeons believe, must contain the same necessary potency as fresh lemon juice. Now the surgeons view the canned meat, vegetables and soup as more than food. To them, and to your men, it is medicine that is saving their lives.

Not a single man aboard the *Erebus* or *Terror* dies during the winter of 1846 to 1847. Both ships survive being stranded in the ice pack.

In May 1847, you, Franklin and Fitzjames decide to send men from the stranded ships to check the ice pack ahead and explore the nearby island. One of the parties follows a straight line to the southeast on the shortest way out of the pack, toward King William Island. Franklin has given instructions to build a cairn — a stack of rocks easily visible from a distance — and to leave behind a message.

Franklin's assumption was simple and well-founded. The ships had followed Admiralty instructions exactly as per the charts. Any future expeditions looking for them would easily find the cairn.

Cairns have been built around the world to mark trails and locations of buried items, for monuments, ceremonies and more.

Walking and sledding across the torturous terrain of the ice pack, it takes Lieutenant Graham Gore and his men five days to cover only 37 km (23 mi.). The message Gore leaves behind in a canister is as follows:

28 of May 1847 H.M.S.hips Erebus and Terror Wintered in the Ice in Lat. 70°5'N Long. 98°23'W Having wintered in 1846-7 [sic] at Beechey Island in Lat 74°43'28"N Long 91°39'15"W

After having ascended Wellington Channel to Lat 77° and returned by the West side of Cornwallis Island.

Sir John Franklin commanding the Expedition. <u>All well</u> *Party consisting of 2 Officers and 6 Men left the ships on Monday 24th May 1847.*

[signed] Gm. Gore, Lieut. [signed] Chas. F. DesVoeux, Mate

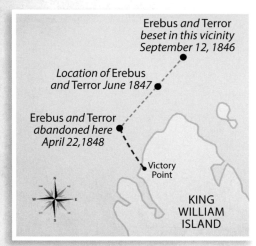

Erebus *and* Terror beset in this vicinity September 12, 1846

Location of Erebus and Terror June 1847

Erebus *and* Terror abandoned here April 22, 1848

Victory Point

KING WILLIAM ISLAND

It took Gore and his men five days to walk and sled only 37 km (23 mi.) from the ships, stuck in ice, to a place known as Victory Point, named in 1831 by James Clark Ross. They left a message in a canister in a cairn they built there, then returned to the ships. Over time, the ships will gradually drift from this location with the movement of pack ice.

All well. That was the essence of Lieutenant Gore's message. Scurvy did not devastate the crew, as you feared. Both ships are still seaworthy.

You hope all will remain well.

But it has been a harsh winter. As June approaches, you doubt there will be a way out of the ice pack this summer. The break-up that would normally come in August may never come. You fear the ships are doomed to be stuck, very slowly drifting with the movement of the pack, but still trapped by the weight of the ice.

As days go by and scouting parties return with little hopeful news, your predicament becomes obvious to all. Yet another horrendous winter ahead, yet another long endurance test. A second winter stuck in the pack ice off King William Land? The prospect devastates morale on both ships.

Worse, coal is disappearing, and so is the food. Burning coal is the most obvious weapon to protect against the cold. But you know that reducing food intake in the frigid Arctic leads to cold, weak and ill men. Better to conserve what coal you can by leaving the fires low and feeding men canned food without heating it.

Then comes another blow to the morale of the crew.

On June 11, barely days after Gore returns, Sir John Franklin dies.

You are now leader of the expedition, with James Fitzjames, the commander of the *Erebus*, second-in-command. The fate of some 120 men now depends on the decisions you make in the next few months.

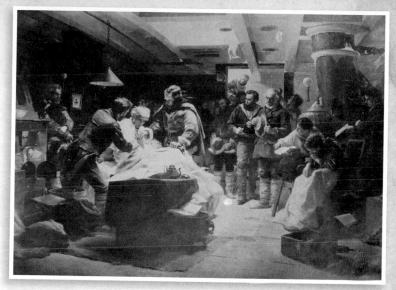

The death of Sir John Franklin, June 11, 1847, as imagined by artist Julius von Payer

Apply Forensic Techniques to
Solve the Mystery

At age 16, Leon Fleisher made his debut with the New York Philharmonic, and was proclaimed as "the pianistic find of the century." His career continued upward — until he lost control of the fourth and fifth fingers of his right hand, which began to curl inward to his palms as his muscles contracted, or tightened.

Neurologists, hand surgeons and orthopedists were unable to help. Fleisher endured X-rays, injections, medications and acupuncture. Nothing helped.

He continued his career, playing with only his left hand but always looking for a way to recover his right hand.

The eventual diagnosis decades later? The involuntary muscle contractions were the result of a misfiring of brain signals, known as

focal dystonia. A sensory processing error.

Although focal dystonia is incurable, a solution was found for his disabling contractions. With a tiny injection of a naturally occurring poison, he was finally able to use his right hand again.

This interests you as a forensic scientist because you discover that instead of targeting the source of the problem — the brain — this potent toxin was applied directly to Fleisher's finger muscles, to be reinjected every six months or so.

Based on what you've learned, from years of experience in analyzing poisons in hair samples and soft tissues, what does your forensic knowledge let you conclude about this substance?

Answer at end of the chapter.

THE SEARCH THEN : A Grave Discovery

William Penny,
August 1851: London, England

Lady Franklin's persistence fascinated the public, as did the continued search for a significant expedition that had simply vanished. The story had become a sort of long-running circus, with players rotating in and out of a spotlight that, most of the time, she held.

She, like the public, had no idea how many of the officers and crew had already perished by the spring of 1850. The vaunted Royal Navy needed the help of a whaler named William Penny to bring back the first hints of disaster.

Penny had already made two previous searches, beginning in 1847, but both times he had been turned back by massive ice packs. His third expedition, which set out in April 1850, was financed by Lady Franklin, who still wanted to believe her husband was alive.

In charge of two ships, Penny joined forces with the Royal Navy and, in the summer of 1850, made a major discovery: weathered wooden markers standing in the permafrost of Beechey Island. Below were the graves of three of Franklin's crew — John Torrington, William Braine and John Hartnell, the men who had died first on the expedition in 1846. Despite careful searching, they could find no written record to indicate anything else about the circumstances of the deaths. They concluded that Erebus and Terror wintered in 1845–1846 in the bay adjacent to Beechey Island, later named Erebus and Terror Bay.

Captain
William Penny

Forced by ice to stay through the winter, it took Penny until 1851 to bring the news back to England. Although there was little else to hint at the expedition's fate, after more than a dozen different searches in the previous few years, including one led by James Clark Ross with *Enterprise* and *Investigator* in 1848, there was finally evidence to point to the route that Franklin had taken.

The Graves, from
The Illustrated London News

After previous extensive efforts to find the ships and crew had brought back little evidence, Penny's news did not bode well for the Admiralty. The expedition had departed with great fanfare, with promises that it would succeed where all other efforts had failed.

What the Admiralty needed now was a major discovery — hopefully, a large group of survivors. Instead, the public now learned about three graves, and no written records and no one rescued.

Public perception was about to get worse for the Admiralty. First came a new story — eventually proved wrong — that Inuit had attacked and murdered the officers and crew.

Then came a more damning story — more damning because it was not simply rumor.

An illustration from Peter Sutherland's *Journal of a Voyage in Baffin's Bay and Barrow Straits in the Years 1850–1851, Performed by H.M. Ships* Lady Franklin *and* Sophia, *Under the Command of Mr. William Penny, in search of the Missing Crews of H.M. Ships* Erebus *and* Terror

Goldner supplied the Admiralty with tens of thousands of pounds of meat packed at his factory in Moldavia, now Romania.

By July 1852, officials had inspected a large sample of the 4535 kg (10 000 lb.) of Stephan Goldner's canned provisions supplied to HMS *Plover* and had forced them to dump overboard the remaining cans. This information eventually reached one of Franklin's relatives, who brought it to the attention of journalists, who in turn knew that any fresh speculation about the Franklin expedition would sell newspapers.

A focus on the spoiled cans put Goldner into the spotlight of the media circus. As a result, the Admiralty faced accusations of allowing Franklin's men to be sent into the Arctic with provisions that had not even been examined for any degree of quality.

Still, no one yet suspected how much of a factor Goldner was in the failure of the expedition.

Elsewhere at the time ...

Down Under

News of the deaths of Torrington, Braine and Hartnell of the *Erebus* and *Terror* revived interest in the lost expedition, but once again, the public's attention had been seized by a gold rush, this time a new one, in Australia. Fortune seekers were greedy for the same type of luck that had fallen upon five men with shovels who together found almost 4 kg (136 oz.) of gold (more than the average birth weight of a baby) in one day, all by barely scraping the surface of the ground. Tent cities grew to populations as large as 40 000. (Convicts who had survived banishment to the penal colonies realized that being shipped from England a year earlier might not have been such a bad thing after all.)

A much less publicized event also occurred in the land Down Under, when John Ridley invented a machine that could strip wheat grains from their stalks, saving countless hours of harvesting by hand. No one knew it at the time, but it began an agricultural revolution with far greater impact on humanity than the much more spectacular gold rush.

John Ridley's stripper harvester

OF SHIPS AND MEN :
A Tale of Two Maps

Inuit Knowledge Keepers, Ice Scientists and the Underwater Archaeology Team, September 2014: O'Reilly Island

These Arctic sea ice images represent real data captured by instruments aboard NASA's Aqua satellite.

In six months, the ice cover of the Northern Hemisphere can grow as much as 9.8 million sq. km (3.8 million sq. mi.). This means the ice pack grows by 2.6 sq. km (1 sq. mi.) roughly every four seconds, or 2340 sq. km (900 sq. mi.) per hour.

It's a lethally fast expansion for anyone trying to navigate through the Northwest Passage. Today, with instant satellite images and helicopters overhead to look for danger, ships still get stuck regularly. No wonder *Erebus* and *Terror* spent months locked in ice pack. But since the ice pack is like a living creature, moving and flowing with the currents, it will also move the ships caught within the ice.

The last known location of the ships was communicated in a message found at Victory Point on King William Island. According to the message, the ships were stuck in ice some 40 km (25 mi.) to the north and west of the shore.

A search mission sponsored by the Canadian government with Inuit and other partners began in 2008. The first five years of searching produced almost no results — some clues on land, but none in the water.

Based on Inuit oral history recorded by Rae and McClintock in the 1850s, Hall in the 1860s and Schwatka in the 1870s, plus the research of Louie Kamookak and David Woodman, the search team had decided on two main search areas.

Guided by Inuit stories and an old Inuit map (see page 53), using modern technology and a "most probable vector" map to understand ice movement, searchers looked for signs of a sunken ship near O'Reilly Island.

The north search area was in Victoria Strait and Alexandra Strait, near where the 138-word note said the ships were abandoned. But ice still blocked Victoria Strait late that summer, so the team focused south, where prospects seemed better.

The south search area, near O'Reilly Island, in the Queen Maud Gulf, was known as Utjulik (Ook-joo-lik), meaning the place of the bearded seals. Inuit told McClintock a ship had wrecked there. They called it the Utjulik wreck.

Like Louie Kamookak, the search team believed the old stories that Inuit had seen a ship near O'Reilly Island, where they saw one dead man plus evidence that men were on the ship not long before they arrived. The team also hoped that the Inuit map drawn for Hall would help lead them to the lost ship.

Side-scan towfish send clear and detailed images of what is in the water to the archaeologist on board the boat towing them.

Modern science helped to confirm the search areas. Parks Canada Underwater Archaeology Team leader Ryan Harris worked with ice scientist Tom Zagon to create a "most probable vector" map, which showed that wind and ice could have carried a ship from Victoria Strait to northeast of O'Reilly Island.

Armed with these two maps and a lot of history, using remote sensing and other technology unavailable to earlier searchers, the team undertook a painstakingly methodical search, launching smaller boats from the expedition ship, scanning the seabed in a grid, block by block.

By September 2014, the team was in their sixth year of searching and had covered more than 1500 sq. km (580 sq. mi.). Although they had just a short search window each year, they had spent more than 16 weeks in the icy waters north, west and south of King William Island.

HMS *Erebus's* recovered davit pintle on top of a cross-section plan of the ship that shows where it came from

When a breakthrough finally came, ironically, it was because of a clue found on land. The break occurred because to search the open waters of the south, they needed a GPS station in place to guide them in straight lines. For that station, they chose a small island northeast of O'Reilly Island.

Captain Andrew Stirling, the helicopter pilot who took the archaeologists and technicians there, landed near an Inuit tent ring they had spotted from the air. While the archaeologists examined the tent ring site, Stirling searched nearby. Then he spotted something rust brown against the gray of the island rocks. Shaped like a hairpin, it was a piece of iron about the length of a human forearm. He called the others over. That was when they saw it had been stamped as Royal Navy property.

A sonar image of HMS *Erebus*, seen from above

Back aboard the main search ship, Jonathan Moore, an archaeologist on the team, identified the object as a davit pintle, part of a device that sailors used to lower and raise small boats alongside a ship. The conclusion was that since the davit piece was too heavy to have blown there, it must have been deposited by moving ice or by someone carrying it.

The next conclusion was breathtaking: that meant the ship must be nearby.

The next day, they shifted their underwater search closer to where the davit pintle was found and, towing a sonar scanner behind their boat, began to scan the nearby seabed. Then came the sonar pings, bouncing off something big and solid.

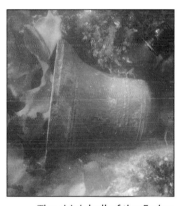

It was a ship, upright, with less than 4.5 m (14 ft.) of clear ocean water above it, disguised by kelp growing around it.

HMS *Erebus*. Ship and ship's bell found on September 2, 2014 — just over 169 years after last seen in Baffin Bay.

The trust in Inuit oral traditions had been vindicated.

The ship's bell of the *Erebus*

 # Mystery SOLVED

Congratulations if you realized Leon Fleisher was able to return to the piano with full use of his right hand thanks to the botulinum toxin.

If ingested, the toxin is so potent that 60 g (a little more than 2 oz.) dispersed in the tiniest of portions is enough to kill one million people.

While *Clostridium botulinum* was recognized over a hundred years earlier for its devastating effects as a food poison, it wasn't until 1980

that a physician, Dr. Alan B. Scott, declared its benefits as a paralyzing agent injected directly into muscles in small doses, where it prevents signals from nerve cells from reaching muscles.

For Fleisher, it meant his fingers would no longer contract into a ball against his palm. And for millions of others, it is now used for vanity. Yes, Botox treatments, to erase wrinkles, are injections of that potent toxin.

EPISODE EIGHT

Abandon Ship

TIMELINE

MAY 1845: THE DOCKS AT GREENHITHE, THAMES RIVER, LONDON, ENGLAND

JULY 1845: DISKO BAY, GREENLAND

AUGUST TO SEPTEMBER 1845: LANCASTER SOUND

SEPTEMBER 1845 TO AUGUST 1846: BEECHEY ISLAND

AUGUST TO SEPTEMBER 1846: PEEL SOUND AND FRANKLIN STRAIT

SEPTEMBER 1846: KING WILLIAM ISLAND

SEPTEMBER 1846 TO JUNE 1847: LAT 70°05' N, LONG 98°23' W

JUNE 1847 TO APRIL 1848: SHIPS LOCKED IN ICE

AUGUST 1848: BOOTH POINT, KING WILLIAM ISLAND

SEPTEMBER 1848: MONTREAL ISLAND, MOUTH OF THE BACK RIVER

LANCASTER SOUND

PEEL SOUND

FRANKLIN STRAIT

BAFFIN ISLAND

Lat 70°05' N, Long 98°23' W

KING WILLIAM ISLAND

HUDSON BAY

NORTH AMERICA

CANADA

PACIFIC OCEAN

UNITED STATES

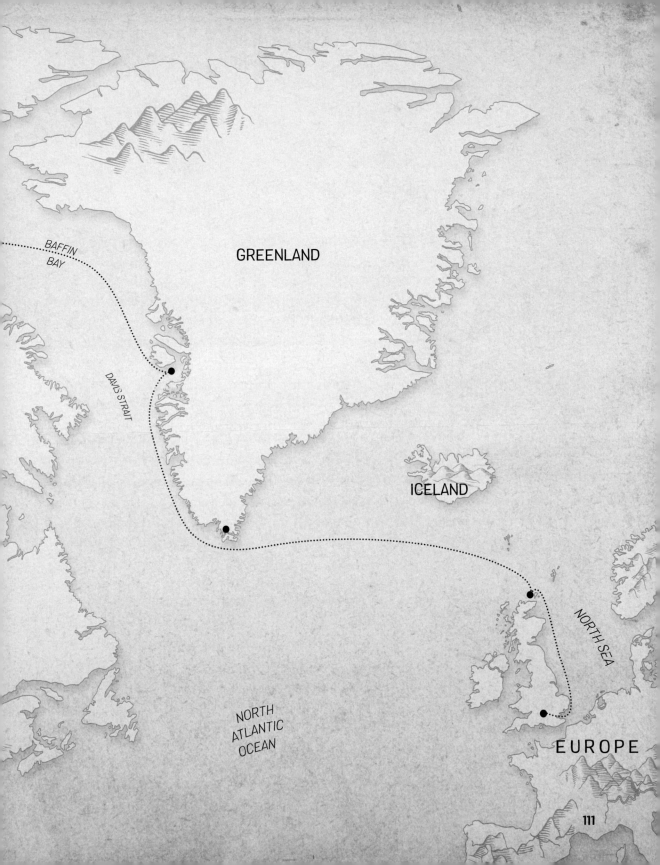

BAFFIN
BAY

DAVIS STRAIT

GREENLAND

ICELAND

NORTH
ATLANTIC
OCEAN

NORTH SEA

EUROPE

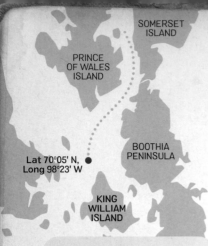

SOMERSET ISLAND

PRINCE OF WALES ISLAND

BOOTHIA PENINSULA

Lat 70°05' N, Long 98°23' W

KING WILLIAM ISLAND

YOUR EXPEDITION :
Mystery Deaths Resume

June 1847 to April 1848:
Ships Locked in Ice

> *"… the total loss by deaths in the Expedition has been to this date 9 officers and 15 men."*
>
> — Francis Crozier, captain of HMS *Terror*, James Fitzjames, captain of HMS *Erebus*, April 25, 1848

It's summer, and not much time has passed since the death of Sir John Franklin. The deceptively bright sun does little to dispel the chill of standing on ice in the shadows of the ships that tower above you. At your feet is a coffin-sized hole your crew cut through the ice, which is so thick that you could lower your entire body before your toes dipped into the deep, dark water.

Four officers on one side of you hold with reverence the canvas-wrapped body of First Lieutenant Graham Gore. The men sing hymns and you offer a prayer.

The officers slide the canvas and its burden into the hole, and with the slightest of splashes it disappears into the depths.

You turn back to the ship, heavy-hearted.

Franklin's death — difficult as it was to the expedition's morale — was at least understandable. Franklin was the oldest man on the expedition, and in poor physical condition. Perhaps the realization that the expedition was trapped for at least another summer and winter — with starvation now a possibility for the men — had triggered this. With his dream of success badly broken, perhaps he was broken. It could have been a heart attack or stroke.

Gore's death, however, is much more devastating because of its horrendous mystery. Forty years old, he had been healthy enough to trek across the pack ice to King William Island and back. Then stomach cramps afflicted him. That was followed by weakness in his muscles that deteriorated to the point of paralysis.

First Lieutenant Graham Gore

His face first. His neck. Then shoulders, arms and legs. Then his lungs. Gore was awake and coherent at the end, but simply unable to move any muscles, including his diaphragm. Helpless, he suffocated to death. All told, it took less than 72 hours for the killer to triumph.

A Funeral on the Ice. The Effect of Paraselenæ — Mock Moons, from Francis Leopold McClintock's *In the Arctic Seas*.

In those 72 hours, nothing could be done to treat him. There was certainly no cure, because the surgeons were helpless in trying to understand what had taken over his body.

In 30 years of Arctic expeditions, no officer of the Royal Navy had ever perished. Then, two, in short succession — Franklin then Gore.

Disturbing as this is, you are the commander and you need to focus on the safety of those still alive. With the ships stuck, you decide that some of the provisions must be moved to land as a precaution in case the ships are crushed during yet another brutal winter entombed in the unyielding ice pack. Perhaps, too, you think but dare not say, sooner or later the ships will need to be abandoned.

The helplessness of the situation worsens.

Over the next 10 months, you watch as 20 more men become sick as Gore did, dying the same horrible way. Including Gore, 21 healthy younger men. Fully one-sixth of the expedition perish.

You and the surgeons are all too aware of the symptoms leading to these deaths. The cramped stomach leads to diarrhea in about half the cases. Dry mouth, blurred vision. Squeaky voice from damaged vocal cords. Difficulty speaking.

For all of them, the same paralysis. Face, neck, shoulders, arms, legs, lungs. Then death from suffocation.

Victory Point and the 138-Word Message

When Lieutenant W. R. Hobson, as part of a search mission led by Captain Francis Leopold McClintock, discovered a cairn at Victory Point on King William Island on May 5, 1859, the message he found was written on a preprinted naval record form that had been supplied by the Admiralty.

Sir Francis Leopold McClintock

It had two entries.

The first entry, handwritten by Fitzjames, was signed and dated by Gore and DesVoeux. It ends with "All Well." The second entry, also handwritten by Fitzjames, was signed by Fitzjames and Crozier. It describes events that happened almost a year after the first entry — the deaths of 9 officers and 15 crew and the abandonment of the ships, still stuck in ice. It also notes the intent to find help by proceeding to Back's Fish River to reach Fort Resolution, the Hudson's Bay Company trading post at Great Slave Lake.

As Captain McClintock famously said, "A sad tale was never told in fewer words."

Artist's conception of opening the cairn at Victory Point, almost 11 years after it was sealed

Here is the transcript of the note:

28 of May 1847

H.M.S.hips Erebus and Terror Wintered in the Ice in Lat. 70°5'N Long. 98°23'W Having wintered in 1846-7 [sic] at Beechey Island in Lat 74°43'28"N Long 91°39'15"W

After having ascended Wellington Channel to Lat 77° and returned by the West side of Cornwallis Island.

Sir John Franklin commanding the Expedition.

<u>*All well*</u>

Party consisting of 2 Officers and 6 Men left the ships on Monday 24th May 1847.

[signed] Gm. Gore, Lieut.

[signed] Chas. F. DesVoeux, Mate

25th April 1848

HMShips Terror and Erebus were deserted on the 22nd April 5 leagues NNW of this having been beset since 12th Sept 1846.

The officers and crews consisting of 105 souls under the command of Captain F. R. M. Crozier landed here — in Lat. 69°37'42" Long. 98°41'

This paper was found by Lt. Irving under the cairn supposed to have been built by Sir James Ross in 1831 — 4 miles to the Northward — where it had been deposited by the late Commander Gore in ~~May~~ *June 1847.*

Sir James Ross' pillar has not however been found and the paper has been transferred to this position which is that in which Sir J. Ross' pillar was erected.

Sir John Franklin died on the 11th of June 1847 and the total loss by deaths in the Expedition has been to this date 9 officers and 15 men.

[signed] F. R. M. Crozier Captain & Senior Offr

And start on tomorrow 26th for Backs Fish River

[signed] James Fitzjames Captain HMS Erebus

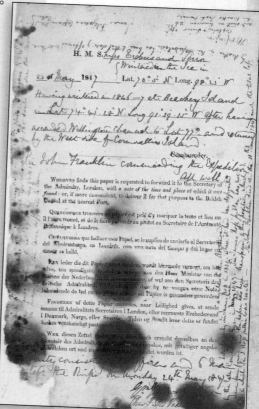

This 138-word message, handwritten on a Navy form letter, was found in a canister in a cairn on King William Island. It included one entry from May 1847 and another from April 1848.

Noon in Mid-Winter, by Lieutenant William Browne. Polar night means darkness all day long. Browne was on the *Enterprise* on James Clark Ross's 1848–1849 voyage in search of the Franklin expedition.

To add to the mystery, when the polar night returns and the ice is too thick to cut for open sea burial, you witness a strange sight from your desk, where yet again, you are dipping pen into ink to record another death of a crew member. The writing itself is not a futile task. Even if all the officers and crew perish, someone will find the ship and the record of events.

As for the strange sight?

The familiar scurry of claws on wood draws your attention. Your idle glance shows that this rat is staggering, as if drunk. You scrape your chair away from the desk, thinking it will flee. Instead, it collapses.

You pick it up by the tail, and its only reaction is a feeble wiggle. You leave your cabin to fling it into the fire in the stove. The cook sees this and shows no surprise. You learn from him that in the lower hold, rats are dying in the dozens. They have been gnawing on the frozen bodies of crewmen stacked in anticipation of burial when summer arrives. Whatever is killing your men is also killing the rats.

Just as grim is the diminishing supply of food and coal. If the ships are to survive months more in the jaws of the ice pack, your only hope is that the water is so open that you can sail instead of relying on the steam engines. All that remains is one week of coal for steaming, forward or backward.

April arrives, a month short of three years since you stood beside Franklin on the docks at Greenhithe as he proudly waved his handkerchief at his wife and the niece who broke your heart. It is two months short of a year since you tipped Franklin's body through a hole in ice into the Arctic waters.

You and the officers and crew are down to half rations because the food supply is so low.

You have no idea how many of your surviving men will be struck down by the mysterious killer that is stalking your crew.

You consult with Fitzjames, but in the end, as commander, you finally make the decision, based on the certainty that you can no longer wait where you are for the slim hope that eventually, open water will free the ships enough to move by sail power.

That leaves the only other option — abandoning your ships while you still have food and your men still have strength.

On foot and sled, then, you could travel east toward Baffin Bay and hope to wave down ships of whaling fleets there in the summer.

Or you can go south to Fort Resolution, a Hudson's Bay trading outpost on Great Slave Lake.

Either choice is near impossible.

East means travel across the mountainous pressure ridges, sheer walls of ice at torturous angles. You'll need to stay on the coastline. That means a trek of more than 1600 km (1000 mi.) and, if you don't arrive before the whaling fleets or possible Royal Navy search ships leave, it will be a wasted journey to a slow death as winter approaches again.

South? The journey is still a daunting 1368 km (850 mi.) and much of it will be upstream on the Back's Fish River (marked on your map as Back or Great Fish River) traveling 83 waterfalls and numerous cascades and rapids through 853 km (530 mi.) of desolate country without a single tree on the banks for most of the journey.

You choose the route to the river, hoping that much of it will be ice free for most of the summer, and that when you arrive at the Hudson's Bay outpost, someone will be there. You also decide there will be a better chance of hunting and fishing along the river. If you are fortunate — and surely you deserve some good fortune — searchers are already traveling from Great Slave Lake by river to search for your expedition.

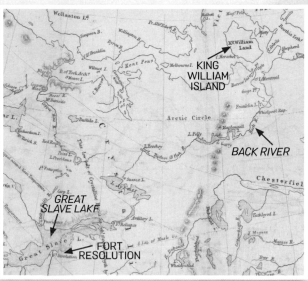

The journey to Fort Resolution, on foot, dragging boats on sledges, then in boats up the river, will take you and your remaining crew over desolate country and treacherous waterfalls — if you can get there. *Map of the North West Part of Canada, Hudson's Bay & Indian Territories*, 1857.

This, of course, is something you have been contemplating for months.

Now you instruct your carpenters to build sleds to carry the smaller boats across the pack ice to the mouth of the river. They are hell to drag across the pack ice, but necessary for survival. You get your men to put cleats in their boots for better grip on ice. You improvise snow goggles. You pack as much food as possible.

You send your men with the equipment in relays across the pack ice to the shoreline of King William Island, to Victory Point. They haul cookstoves and tents, clothing and food. They even have brass curtain rods and a lightning conductor. They have instructions to put up the tents to make it a semi-permanent campsite, a place to recover before moving on.

Some of the crew's personal items, later found by McClintock

Finally, on April 22, with the last of your crew, you take the final steps to abandon ships.

Officers and crew are allowed to pack personal items — photos, family mementos — with their gear. You count down each hour by tolling the ship's bronze bell. You make a final inspection and then order the hatchways secured and sealed. You raise the flags to show the Royal Navy colors. You order the bell clapper tied in place so that it will not toll on an empty ship. You gather the officers and crew and say a prayer.

Then you walk away on the ice, leaving the flags to flap in the wind that cuts into your face. You leave behind the rats, the nightmares of nights in polar darkness and the heavy anxiety of wondering from hour to hour if the ice pack will crush you.

When you arrive at King William Island after an exhausting trek across the ice, another man dies. This hits harder than all the others. Lieutenant John Irving is one of your junior officers and a close friend. You make sure Irving is buried with care, placing a colored silk handkerchief as a pillow under his head, and including a medal and officer's gold buttons.

Now 10 out of 24 officers have died. Mysteriously and with no warning. You make a new decision: to immediately leave and hope for the best.

When you order the men to pack up the canned provisions you will need for your march south, however, you still have no idea you are taking your killers with you.

Artist Julius von Payer created a series of four scenes from the Franklin expedition. This painting shows the men abandoning their vessels.

Apply Forensic Techniques to
Solve the Mystery

As a forensic scientist, you would certainly recognize the name Colin Pitchfork. He made history in your field as the first murderer to be caught and found guilty through DNA analysis.

This was barely 30 years ago, and since then, DNA profiling has gone mainstream, from courtrooms to television shows.

Naturally, this relatively new science has helped solve many of the questions around the Franklin expedition. DNA from the skeletal remains of sailors is now being used to try to identify those on the crew list. All the bones discovered — many of them scattered because of animal scavengers — point to 24 individuals.

One unexpected test result has led some researchers to speculate that four of the remains came from women.

Hannah Snell joined the Corps of Royal Marines in 1745 and served with them, undiscovered, for five years.

Women!

Furthermore, those bones contain European DNA, which rules out the possibility that the bones belonged to Inuit women.

This finding contradicts everything that historians know about the crew.

As a forensic scientist, what are your conclusions about the bones and DNA of those crew members?

Answer at end of the chapter.

THE SEARCH THEN : Villainy Revealed

Stephan Goldner, February 1852: London, England

Beginning with his contract of December 28, 1844, until 1851, Stephan Goldner supplied the Royal Navy with 1 243 745 kg (2 741 988 lb.) of preserved meat. There is a terrible irony in the fact that the Admiralty was able to determine this number so precisely, yet really had no idea of what the conditions were like in Goldner's factory.

First, with the canning industry less than 30 years old, the process was far from perfect. Done right, making the can itself was a 16-step process. But this was too expensive for Goldner and took too much time. Each shortcut — including the addition of arsenic to the lead solder that was melted to hold the cans together — saved him money. Even then, he needed to take another shortcut to meet the demands of his contract for the Franklin expedition. Instead of supplying 9000 kg (20 000 lb.) of meat in 0.45 kg (1 lb.) cans, he could supply larger and much cheaper 4 kg (9 lb.) cans.

Cans were dipped in boiling water to cook the food before sealing them. A 4 kg can demanded a far longer time to raise the temperature of the contents high enough to kill bacteria.

This 1852 etching of a meat factory linked to Goldner appeared in an *Illustrated London News* story that praised the contents of the "canisters" as excellent.

Compared to metal, food is an extremely inefficient conductor of heat. The large cans made it almost certain that uncooked cold spots remained in the center.

As for the bacteria that should have been killed by heat?

Livestock was packed into pens where urine and manure ran freely. The animals were slaughtered with dull knives that pounded bacteria into the meat. The raw food itself was untended and unrefrigerated, attacked by rats, flies, roaches and pigeons that all left behind droppings to mix with the food. Nor were the laborers concerned about what went into the food. They were under pressure to pack as many cans as possible. Animal guts and bones were as likely to be used as meat itself.

Sledge Parties Departing from Resolute *and* Intrepid *to Search for Franklin, 1853.* This, the last big search mission sponsored by the Admiralty, was not provisioned by Goldner.

This raw food was packed into unsterilized cans by unskilled laborers in filthy clothing that carried lice and fleas, laborers who contracted diarrhea from sharing a single outhouse and never washed their hands, laborers who coughed and spread the tuberculosis and influenza and pneumonia that they picked up by living packed in rooming houses.

The beginning of the end for Goldner came in February 1852, when the British House of Commons began a full-scale investigation that revealed Goldner's villainy. A portion of the report noted that cans often contained: "pieces of heart, roots of tongues, pieces of palates, pieces of tongues, coagulated blood, pieces of liver, ligaments of the throat, pieces of intestines."

And villainy it was, for Goldner was providing canned poison. The evidence was there in the cans distorted with bulges as bacteria inside multiplied.

Cooked for long enough at a high heat, these bacteria would be destroyed, leaving food that was horrible to eat but safe enough. For a crew running low on coal, eating straight from the can outdoors in cold weather, it was deadly.

Some say that the canned meat Goldner supplied to the Franklin expedition was of better quality than the meat inspected in later years. Others say Goldner's employees disliked him and deliberately sabotaged the product they were making. Some claim that the Admiralty needed to blame someone, and a "foreigner" like Goldner made a good scapegoat.

For his crimes and greed, Goldner faced bankruptcy. In typical villainous style, he vanished before the punishment arrived. History does not know what became of him.

But the remains of the officers and crew who died from the potent toxins released by bacteria inside Goldner's cans of food leave a grim and unforgettable legacy, later unraveled by a full understanding of the specific bacteria itself.

Goldner-supplied cans left behind by the expedition

Elsewhere at the time …

An Arresting Fashion Statement

Even as the scandal of Goldner's treachery made headlines across the Atlantic, the proper citizens of Boston were aghast at events closer to home, in their own city, caused by the 17-year-old daughter of a New York City police officer.

Her crime? Wearing pants as she walked city streets. Each time Emma Snodgrass was arrested — yup, arrested — and sent home to her father, she would return to Boston to be arrested again.

Soon enough, her exploits became national news, and as one newspaper reported, she "disturbed the equanimity of the sleepy magistracy in the eastern cities." Translation: A woman wearing pants was upsetting for court judges.

Apparently delighted by the attention, she began to travel across the country to face a similar fate in other cities. She was last known to be arrested in Cleveland in June 1853.

After that, Snodgrass disappeared from public sight. Imagine how much easier it would have been for her to become a sensation with an Instagram account.

OF SHIPS AND MEN : Death in Paradise

Dr. David Cooper and Team,
September 2018: Royal Naval Hospital, Antigua

> "Human bone turns over, it changes, it sort of rebuilds itself, even in adulthood — but at a very slow rate. So what that means is that if the individuals in the expedition had lots of lead within their bones, it really implies it was there before the expedition."
>
> — Dr. David Cooper

In October 1987, *History Today* magazine published a headline that summarized a new understanding of a major contributor to the Franklin expedition disaster: "Canned Food Sealed Icemen's Fate."

The summary of the article promised readers an answer based on the forensic science of the time:

Dramatic evidence that lead poisoning was a key element in the failure of Sir John Franklin's 1845 Arctic expedition has come from the result of postmortems conducted on the preserved bodies of three of Franklin's crewmen taken from their frozen graves on Beechey Island in the Canadian Arctic.

Yet science — forensic science included — is a discipline that continuously tests old theories against new evidence. In fact, the word "forensic" comes from the Latin term *forensis*, which means public debate or discussion. "Forensic science" usually refers to the application of scientific knowledge and methods to legal problems, especially criminal matters. But scientific knowledge and methods can change and produce new results for old puzzles. In 2013 and 2016, technological advances in forensic science provided such new evidence, and meant Beattie's once-accepted theory needed a thorough re-examination.

In 2018, Dr. David Cooper, an expert in cell biology, had a team prepared to examine the bones once again — but not only the

A "bone detective" examines deer bones that have been frozen and thawed to be able to learn more about human bones.

bones of the crew of the Franklin expedition. They decided the conclusive answer might be found in comparing them with bones of other sailors who also lived in the mid-1800s.

Back then, the Royal Navy and its fleet of 500 ships dominated — and roamed — the oceans of the globe. The Admiralty maintained hospitals around the world specifically to care for and treat the officers and crew of their fleets.

One such hospital was on an island in the West Indies.

English Harbour, Antigua, where the Royal Navy established a base in the 1700s

There probably could not be a more vivid contrast between the Arctic endured by Franklin's sailors and the island of Antigua in the West Indies of the Caribbean. In the north — towering masses of ice, howling blizzards, nights that lasted for months. In the Caribbean islands — balmy breezes, deep green fronds of palm trees and white beaches of sand leading to inviting warm waters.

Even in paradise, though, sailors suffer injuries and get sick. And die.

While the officers and crew of the *Erebus* and *Terror* could turn only to the surgeons and assistant surgeons for help, in Antigua, on the south end of the island, overlooking English Harbour, the Royal Navy had set up a hospital. Although it had once been destroyed by a hurricane, it was rebuilt in 1783 and remained open until just a few decades before the Franklin expedition departed England in 1845.

This stamp features Lord Admiral Nelson and HMS *Boreas* at anchor in "Nelson's Dockyard," Antigua.

While the first few sailors who died on the Franklin expedition had their bodies placed into permafrost, their counterparts in Antigua were given resting places beneath warm earth scented with blossoms.

If the Royal Navy was good at one thing, that was meticulous record keeping. Ship logs kept detailed notes, payroll receipts were accurate to the penny, letters to the Admiralty were archived, burial records were painstakingly precise.

Dr. Cooper realized that the ancient burials at the hospital grounds overlooking English Harbour could give them exactly the comparison they needed. They learned that lead levels in the bones of those sailors matched the levels found in the bones of fellow sailors in the north. Across all spectrums, sailors had the same exposure to lead during their lifetimes.

Conclusion: lead poisoning was not a factor in the mysterious deaths of the sailors of the Franklin expedition.

What, then, killed them? They left England as strong, healthy men. They had plenty of food.

Were the tins of food the culprit, but for a different reason than Owen Beattie had first proposed some 30 years earlier?

The bodies of John Torrington, John Hartnell and William Braine had provided the only soft tissue and the only hair, fingernails and toenails available for forensics to examine. These soft tissues showed they had died from a combination of tuberculosis and pneumonia, long before uncooked food from the cans would have poisoned their crewmates.

Was there anything else in the soft tissue that forensic science could use to help solve this medical mystery? Especially since the crewmates who died later left behind no soft tissue, as their bodies, exposed to the elements and scavengers, had been stripped to the bone for over a century.

By tradition, sailors on Royal Navy ships received a tot of rum once a day. Scientists believe lead-contaminated rum contributed to high levels of lead found in the bones of the men in the Royal Navy cemetery in Antigua.

Mystery SOLVED

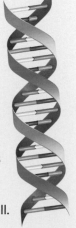

Congratulations if you decide you are not yet able to come to a firm conclusion.

Despite the accuracy that DNA analysis can give, you acknowledge as a forensic scientist that the age and deterioration of the DNA could simply be giving a false result. These bones could in fact belong to men.

On the other hand, there are many stories about women who disguised themselves as men and served in the Royal Navy, their true identities going undiscovered for years. Given the well-documented list of officers and crew, you cannot conclude that women were among them. While the speculation is intriguing, it is just that.

Nevertheless, your forensic inquiries have begun to come up with valuable answers to the mysteries of the expedition that are not speculation at all.

EPISODE NINE

The Unthinkable

TIMELINE

MAY 1845: THE DOCKS AT GREENHITHE, THAMES RIVER, LONDON, ENGLAND

JULY 1845: DISKO BAY, GREENLAND

AUGUST TO SEPTEMBER 1845: LANCASTER SOUND

SEPTEMBER 1845 TO AUGUST 1846: BEECHEY ISLAND

AUGUST TO SEPTEMBER 1846: PEEL SOUND AND FRANKLIN STRAIT

SEPTEMBER 1846: KING WILLIAM ISLAND

SEPTEMBER 1846 TO JUNE 1847: LAT 70°05' N, LONG 98°23' W

JUNE 1847 TO APRIL 1848: SHIPS LOCKED IN ICE

AUGUST 1848: BOOTH POINT, KING WILLIAM ISLAND

SEPTEMBER 1848: MONTREAL ISLAND, MOUTH OF THE BACK RIVER

LANCASTER SOUND

PEEL SOUND

FRANKLIN STRAIT

BAFFIN ISLAND

Lat 70°05' N, Long 98°23' W

KING WILLIAM ISLAND

Booth Point

HUDSON BAY

NORTH AMERICA

CANADA

UNITED STATES

PACIFIC OCEAN

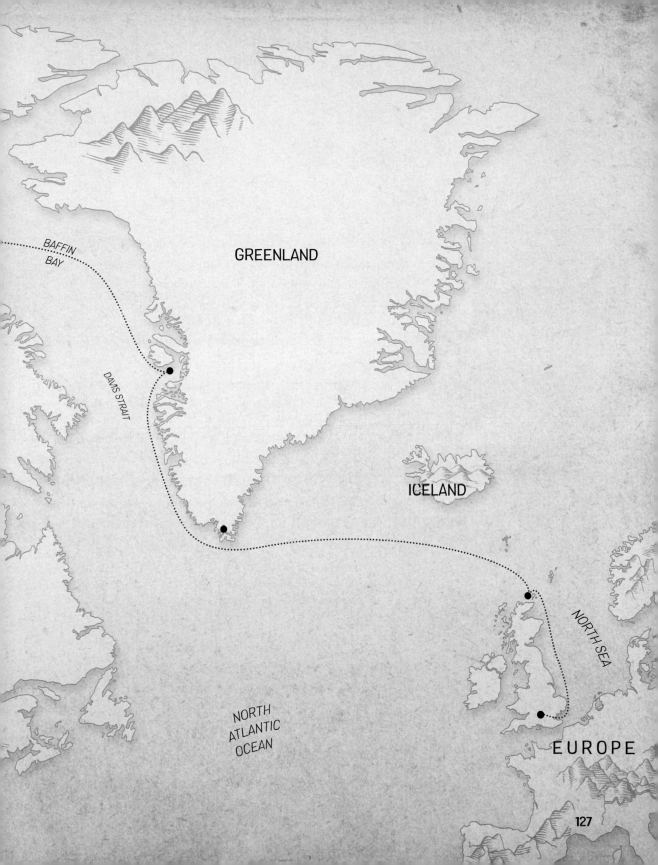

BAFFIN
BAY

GREENLAND

DAVIS STRAIT

ICELAND

NORTH SEA

NORTH
ATLANTIC
OCEAN

EUROPE

KING
WILLIAM
ISLAND

Booth Point

YOUR EXPEDITION :
Northwest Passage Found
August 1848: Booth Point, King William Island

25th April 1848 HMShips Terror and Erebus were deserted on 22nd April 5 leagues NNW of this having been beset since 12th Sept 1846.
The officers and crews, consisting of 105 souls, under the command of Captain F. R. M. Crozier landed here — in Lat. 69°37'42" Long. 98°41' …

[signed] FRM Crozier Captain and Senior Officer

And start on tomorrow 26th for Backs Fish River

[signed] James Fitzjames Captain HMS *Erebus*

Again, you race against the arrival of a polar winter. This time, however, the race is on foot. From Victory Point, you leave behind some food and the heaviest of clothes. You take the shortest route, across the ice pack of an inlet. There are 105 of you, and your pace is agonizingly slow in the truest sense of the word.

Your men are in harnesses like sled dogs. They drag heavy boats filled with food and gear. Each new slab of ice presents a new challenge. Try to drag up and over? Or attack with pickax and shovels? Every 20 steps, they need to stop and suck air into their lungs to rest. At times, it takes an hour to move 45 m (150 ft).

You sink to hips in snow one moment, then plunge through thin ice the next, jerked back to safety by the harness.

Toes begin to freeze solid. Amputation is the only choice, using a snipper to cut through frozen flesh and joints.

Worse, the land around you is horribly bleak and devoid of life. There are no Inuit in this area because they avoid the western flank of the island for this very reason.

You reach an inlet. The 10 km (6 mi.) distance through the slabs of broken ice is still a better alternative than going all the way around on land. During that crossing another officer and crew member die. There is no time for the luxury of a careful burial.

Another 19 km (12 mi.) south of that, another officer dies: Lieutenant Henry LeVesconte. Now the officers' death rate is closing in on 50 percent.

Lieutenant Henry LeVesconte

Two weeks of hellish travel later, you are down to 13 officers and 80 crew. All of you are starving. Pulling the boats is near impossible, but to leave them behind is a sure death sentence; without them, you won't be able to cross open waters ahead.

Finally, you admit that some of your men will not be able to do the impossible.

You make another decision.

On the shores of Erebus Bay, you divide the officers and crew. The weakest will stay behind to try to return to Victory Point and the provisions there, which include some remaining coal and heavy clothing. You instruct these officers and crew to survive winter as best as possible, and to wait for you to come back with rescuers after you reach Great Slave Lake.

The sorrow you felt at being spurned by the woman you love is nothing compared to the difficulty in saying goodbye to these officers and crew. You have shared three full years together, surviving all that the Arctic has thrown at you.

Those left behind, expecting to die before rescue, give personal items to the stronger men who forge ahead, hoping that at least these items will reach their loved ones back in England. In return, those continuing south give items for safekeeping, like gold watches that will not help them during the race toward Great Slave Lake and Fort Resolution.

You and the remaining crew begin to drag the boats farther south and leave the others behind. You have rifles, bullets and powder. While you hope to shoot migratory birds, the island appears to be barren of game animals.

This painting, *The Crew of HMS* Terror *Saving the Boats and Provisions on the Night of 15th March (1837),* by George Hyde Chambers, was based on George Back's account of the Frozen Strait Expedition, 1836–1837, which Back commanded. It dramatizes the scene after *Terror* hit an iceberg in March 1837.

Sledges were built large enough to carry boats as long as 8.5 m (28 ft.). More than 20 men might be needed to pull a boat loaded with supplies.

At the height of summer, you begin to hate the sun that you missed so badly during polar nights. Its reflection off the snow and ice blinds you and burns your skin into blisters. When it loses strength at the end of each day, the sweat in your coat freezes and constricts you to the point of near paralysis.

By mid-August, against all odds and as a testament to your willpower, you have traveled 130 km (80 mi.) with your boats across some of the harshest terrain on the planet.

What Happens to a Human Body During Starvation?

After you eat, your digestive process turns food into the glucose that provides energy for your body. If you don't eat for 8 to 12 hours, your glucose supply is essentially gone, and your body finds a way to make an alternative energy source — glycogen — stored in your liver and muscles. When this is depleted, your body turns to amino acids — a protein — for energy.

After about three days without food, your body shifts into starvation mode to try to preserve muscle tissue. It begins to burn your fat reserves. Obviously, the more fat your body has, the longer you can live without food intake.

Go so long without food that your fat reserves are gone, and your body is unable to supply necessary nutrients to your heart and lungs, which begin to shrink.

In the late stages of starvation, your body waits till it has no choice but to begin to break down your muscle tissue to draw energy from the proteins. That leads you to hallucinations and convulsions. Eventually, when it breaks down protein from your heart muscle, the heart stops beating.

How long can you go without food?

That depends entirely on how much energy you use each day. Lying on a bed at room temperature and sipping water means you could live weeks, even months.

For the officers and crew of the *Erebus* and *Terror*, however, theirs was a much different situation, as they fought to drag heavy sleds over hazardous terrain in icy weather, a situation that demanded hundreds of extra calories a day to provide them with extra energy.

The only blessing is that the mysterious deaths have ended. No more stomach cramps followed by paralysis.

You are too distracted by other deaths, however, to wonder about this. Men are dying from starvation and scurvy and frostbite. If you did have time to think about it, you might realize that the mysterious deaths ended after the last of the canned food had been eaten.

All that matters to you now is finding food so that you and your officers and crew can consume enough calories to find warmth and energy. All that remains to eat is some chocolate, tea and the leather uppers of your shoes.

As if this isn't enough to endure, as you reach the shoreline at the place known as Booth Point, you come to a bitter realization, confirmed by earlier reports from the narrower sections of Simpson Strait.

Beyond the ice-choked strait, although hardly visible at this distance, is mainland. King William Land is not a peninsula but a large island. If the water was open, this would be an east–west passage across the Arctic.

Yes, this is the fabled Northwest Passage. Had ice conditions been different, had Franklin been able to send the *Erebus* and *Terror* down the eastern side of King William Island — a land mass that prevented the ice pack from jamming the waters — your ships would have made safe passage to here. And you would not have been stuck in the ice pack for a winter, then a summer, then a winter.

This discovery, however, matters little if you don't survive now, for the knowledge will disappear with your deaths. Indeed, fighter that you are, you doubt you will survive. Not without food.

Your men have legs swollen with scurvy, feet with no toes, and their bodies are near skeletons. The only way to survive is by somehow finding a new source of nutrients to give the men energy and ease the scurvy.

When yet another of the crew falls down and dies, you make your most horrendous decision. For the answer is face down in front of you.

From Booth Point, you cannot easily see across the Simpson Strait to the mainland Adelaide Peninsula. Most maps still call the land you are on King William Land, yet it is indeed an island.

Apply Forensic Techniques to
Solve the Mystery

Thirty-four shallow graves and 11 bodies found with shattered bones or crushed skulls. This was the initial discovery at Zeleny Yar in the Siberian Arctic. Forensic science indicated the bodies had been buried sometime between 1200 CE and 1300 CE. Some of the bodies were wrapped in birch bark. Five adult males were found mummified, cocooned in animal furs and with copper plates like armor on their bellies and throats. All the bodies were buried in alignment with feet pointing to a nearby river. Did this have religious significance?

As more bodies were discovered in burial sites — 47 so far — it took a cross-section of experts to examine the evidence, consider the research and provide arguments for any conclusions. Archaeologists paid attention to the external artifacts, such as iron combat knives, bronze figurines and several bronze bowls that originated in Persia.

Forensic scientists relied on CT scans and microscopic examinations of soft tissues and bones, along with DNA analysis. As one of those forensic scientists, you are excited to realize your finds from well-preserved inner organs are similar to those of mummified specimens discovered in other countries. But there is a difference, too, and you realize that the presence of copper has significance.

However, given the forest growth here at the edge of the Arctic Circle in Siberia, you note something else that allows you to make the almost certain conclusion that one of the bodies was buried in the year 1282.

So, with help from your archaeologist friends, what exciting conclusions are you able to share about this site?

Answer at end of the chapter.

A mummy from Zeleny Yar

THE SEARCH THEN : A Gold Cap Band

John Rae, July 1854: Pelly Bay, Arctic

"During my journey over ice and snow this spring, with the view of completing the survey of the west shore of the Boothia … I met with Esquimax in Pelly Bay, from one of whom I learned that a party of white men, (Kablounus) had perished from want of food, some distance to the westward and not far beyond a large river containing my falls and rapids."

— John Rae's report to the Admiralty

John Rae admired the Inuit and learned from their ways.

In later summer and fall of 1853, British attention shifted to the unfolding military conflict that became known as the Crimean War. Lasting until 1856, it saw Russia challenging an alliance of countries that included the United Kingdom.

Lady Franklin, however, was determined to keep the search going. The public viewed her as the grieving wife of a naval hero. She raised money and spent much of her own fortune to outfit ship after ship in search of the lost officers and crew.

The first real indications of the fate of the expedition came by land, not ship. Because it wasn't the report they wanted, Lady Franklin refused to believe it was accurate.

For in 1854, six years after teaming with Sir John Richardson on the first overland search for Franklin, John Rae was in the north again, surveying a section of the Arctic for the Hudson's Bay Company, but also, of course, on the lookout for evidence of the expedition's fate. Of astonishing significance was his encounter near Pelly Bay (now Kugaaruk) with a group of Inuit, known in that era as Esquimaux. He saw that one of the men wore a gold cap band that could not have come from anywhere else but the Franklin expedition.

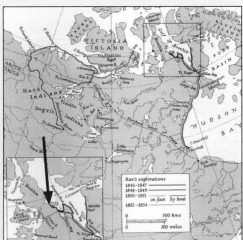

In 1854, Rae searched from Repulse Bay (Naujaat) to King William Island (yellow route on inset map, left).

These Inuit passed along a story about a party of 35 or so white men who had died of starvation near the mouth of the Back River, on the south side of the strait separating

The Back River, originally Great Fish River, got its name from explorer George Back.

King William Island from the mainland. (The Back River, or Haningayok, was then known as Back's Fish River in honor of George Back, who traveled it in 1834. Before that it was known as Great Fish River.) Other Inuit confirmed this, and the clincher, at least from Rae's perspective, was the many objects the Inuit carried that were also easily identified as belonging to Franklin and his men. For example, they had silver forks and spoons that had belonged to Franklin and Crozier.

They also told Rae that most of the men had been thin and weak. Their leader, they said, was a middle-aged man, tall and broad. For Rae, this was a description fitting Francis Crozier. Inuit told Rae they called this leader by the name Aglukkaq.

Rae sent a report to the Admiralty, urging them to send an expedition up the river to search for other signs of the officers and crew.

It would seem, all these long years later, that this major discovery had revealed the expedition's fate. It happened shortly after the Admiralty had finally declared in January 1854 that it would strike from the books all names of the officers and crew of the *Erebus* and *Terror*.

Rae's letter outraged Lady Franklin, for it included information she found so abhorrent that she immediately began a publicity campaign to discredit Rae. The greatest novelist of the day, Charles Dickens, wrote magazine pieces to support her and condemn Rae, as well as cast doubt on the Inuit testimony.

The outrage came from a single sentence in Rae's written description of his findings, published in the *Times* of London, Monday, October 23, 1854:

In 1854, Rae met an Inuk who wore a gold cap band, from a Royal Navy cap like this one. The Inuit said they had found it along with other objects at a camp near the mouth of the Back River, where a group of European men had died of starvation. What is left of the original cap band is in the collection of the National Maritime Museum in Greenwich, London.

From the mutilated state of many of the corpses and the contents of the kettles, it is evident that our wretched countrymen had been driven to the last resource — cannibalism — as a means of prolonging existence.

In Victorian England, it was an affront to suggest that honorable countrymen with high Christian morals would engage in something so evil. Dickens called it "the wild tales of a herd of savages."

Making it easier to discredit the Inuit testimony was Rae's admission that they themselves had not seen the men or the bodies but had heard it from other Inuit who lived farther west.

For many, the expedition's fate remained shrouded in Arctic mystery. And just as fascinating as ever.

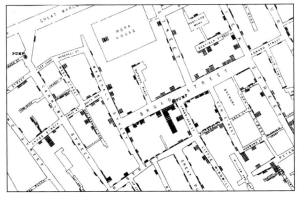

Elsewhere at the time …

A Dot Map and Pump without a Handle

Reports of cannibalism rocked London but had to compete for public interest with an outbreak of cholera in the Soho area. The disease led to death from dehydration, caused by severe vomiting and watery diarrhea. Over 600 people succumbed before it ended. And that ending came only when a physician named John Snow refused to accept the common belief that cholera and plague were caused by breathing bad air.

He put together a dot map showing the homes of all the victims who died during a London outbreak of cholera that had killed hundreds. He traced the source to the center of that map, a public well. He convinced the local council to remove the pump's handle. The outbreak abruptly ended. Later it would be discovered that the well had been dug near an old cesspool, which collected human waste, and the water was contaminated by sewage. Soon, public health policy in big cities around the world would focus on the importance of germ-free water, saving countless hundreds of thousands of future lives.

OF SHIPS AND MEN : Ghost Ship

Sammy Kogvik, September 2016: Terror Bay

> *"Terror Bay is known for many spooky encounters in the past. It gives me shivers."*
>
> — Louie Kamookak

Because of the single 138-word note found at Victory Point on King William Island, what is known for certain is that both the *Erebus* and *Terror* were trapped in ice off the northwest coast of King William Island. In April of 1848, expedition leader Francis Crozier began offloading provisions from the ships, directing his crew to haul them to a base at Victory Point. From there, all the men began to march south, hoping to reach Back's Fish River (now the Back River) and to follow it upstream to a trading post at the eastern end of Great Slave Lake, in what is now the Northwest Territories.

Established Inuit oral history also provided strong evidence that some of the men returned to the *Erebus*, and either sailed it or stayed in it as it drifted to where it was found in 2014, just off O'Reilly Island.

As for the *Terror*, the same Inuit testimony held that it had become a ghost ship. We can

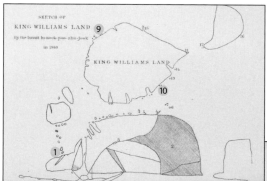

SKETCH OF KING WILLIAMS LAND
By the Innuit In-nook-poo-zhu-jook in 1869

KING WILLIAMS LAND

Compare the map In-nook-poo-zhee-jook drew for Hall in 1869 and the modern-day map. Numbers on the Inuit map refer to places and events the Inuk described as noted here (not all shown):

1 One of Franklin's ships believed sunk here

9 Two smaller boats found here

10 Mutilated remains of five white men found here

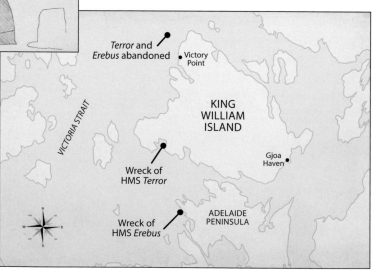

Terror and Erebus abandoned • Victory Point

KING WILLIAM ISLAND

VICTORIA STRAIT

Gjoa Haven •

Wreck of HMS *Terror*

Wreck of HMS *Erebus*

ADELAIDE PENINSULA

speculate that, with the *Erebus* crowded, bodies of crewmen who had died during the winter were transferred to the frozen hold of the sister ship. Before abandoning the ship, Crozier would have given orders to close the hatches and leave it in an orderly fashion.

That could only be true if during the same ice thaw that eventually set the *Erebus* free, the *Terror* had either drifted south or been crewed on its own journey, with bodies perhaps given a sea burial along the away.

Although Inuit knowledge had been proven correct with the discovery of the *Erebus*, there were not as many clues to the location of what searchers called the northern wreck. Some believed the *Terror* could have been wrecked and its remains scattered in deep waters anywhere south of the northwest coast of King William Island. Their search area was not tightly defined.

Strengthened by Francis Hall's record of Inuit stories, however, Louie Kamookak, David Woodman and others believed they had proof of a likely location. From the Inuit, they heard descriptions of silhouettes of a masted ship that could be seen in the springtime in waters much earlier named after the long-lost HMS *Terror* — Terror Bay. Modern-day Inuit had seen the wavy outline of a ship below the waters when flying overhead.

Sammy Kogvik

And when an Inuk named Sammy Kogvik decided to share a story he'd been keeping for years, searchers for the *Terror* had their final clue.

Sammy had signed on as part of the crew of the Arctic Research Foundation vessel *Martin Bergmann*, one of a three-ship expedition that had been given only a nine-day window in 2016 to search for the *Terror*.

Adrian Schimnowski

Kogvik had little trust for outsiders, but Adrian Schimnowski, a co-captain of the ship, was a good listener, and at one point Kogvik told the captain about the camera he had lost some seven or eight years earlier.

Kogvik's story began with a description of crossing Terror Bay over sea ice by snowmobile with a fishing buddy. They'd seen a pole sticking out of the ice, the height of a tall man, thick enough that he could give it a bear hug while his buddy took a photo on Kogvik's camera. Kogvik's father-in-law, following their trail, reported that he, too, had seen the same thick pole. He also told Kogvik stories about a sunken ship from the old days. Trouble was, Kogvik had forgotten to zip his pocket shut and he'd lost the camera. To him, this was a bad omen, so he rarely shared his story.

Schimnowski and the team on his ship agreed it was worth a detour to Terror Bay for a short search. The *Bergmann* changed direction and arrived early the next morning. By 6:00 a.m., search boats were in the water. By 8:20 a.m. the next day, the crew had agreed to give up. The *Terror* was not there.

With boats back on board, Schimnowski set the autopilot on the *Bergmann*, using a different route than the one he'd taken into the bay because deeper waters on the way out offered safety, and they were finished searching. But then the water below the ship suddenly became shallower because of a shoal. That was when the ship's sonar began to ping.

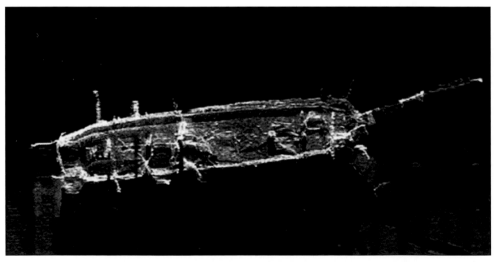

Shortly after the discovery in Terror Bay, the Parks Canada Underwater Archeology Team arrived to scan the wreck, examine the historical and archaeological evidence, and scientifically confirm its identity. This side-scan sonar image of HMS *Terror* shows the details of the bowsprit, masts and placement of the helm.

Yes.

HMS *Terror*. One hundred and seventy-one years after it left the Greenhithe docks with Francis Rawdon Moira Crozier at the helm, the world knew of its final resting place, in just under 24 m (79 ft.) of water.

Today, to protect the sites of the two shipwrecks and allow for further research, their exact locations have not yet been shared with the public. Together, they make up the Wrecks of HMS *Erebus* and HMS *Terror* National Historic Site, cooperatively managed by Inuit and Parks Canada. But visitors to the Nattilik Heritage Centre in Gjoa Haven, Nunavut, can learn about the essential role of Inuit knowledge, passed down from one generation to the next, in finding *Erebus* and *Terror*.

HMS *Terror*'s wheel, found in its original location on the upper deck

Mystery SOLVED

Congratulations if you realized that the presence of copper meant the mummification was not deliberate, and that the bronze bowls that originated in Persia are significant!

The site is known as the Zeleny Yar Necropolis. Like other necropolises — large designed cemeteries — it is a sign of a highly organized society. Indeed, the elaborate burials point to differences in social classes.

You know, thanks to your forensic training, that three factors caused the accidental mummification of the bodies. The first two are obvious: permafrost and sandy soil, with little moisture in it to encourage decay. It's the presence of copper, however, that added a third and necessary ingredient, for copper prevents oxidation.

You didn't need forensic science to determine that one burial took place in 1282 AD, but only common sense and the patience to count tree rings, the circular lines seen when a tree is cut across.

The Persian bowls, however, are the most intriguing. There are no recognized trade routes through Siberia. Essentially, what you are proposing as a forensic scientist is that these bodies indicate that this is a long-lost medieval civilization — so far to the north that it staggers the imagination — that could have been an Arctic outpost of the Persian empire.

EPISODE TEN
Last Days

LANCASTER SOUND

PEEL SOUND

FRANKLIN STRAIT

BAFFIN ISLAND

KING WILLIAM ISLAND

MONTREAL ISLAND

HUDSON BAY

NORTH AMERICA

CANADA

PACIFIC OCEAN

UNITED STATES

TIMELINE

MAY 1845: THE DOCKS AT GREENHITHE, THAMES RIVER, LONDON, ENGLAND

JULY 1845: DISKO BAY, GREENLAND

AUGUST TO SEPTEMBER 1845: LANCASTER SOUND

SEPTEMBER 1845 TO AUGUST 1846: BEECHEY ISLAND

AUGUST TO SEPTEMBER 1846: PEEL SOUND AND FRANKLIN STRAIT

SEPTEMBER 1846: KING WILLIAM ISLAND

SEPTEMBER 1846 TO JUNE 1847: LAT 70°05' N, LONG 98°23' W

JUNE 1847 TO APRIL 1848: SHIPS LOCKED IN ICE

AUGUST 1848: BOOTH POINT, KING WILLIAM ISLAND

SEPTEMBER 1848: MONTREAL ISLAND, MOUTH OF THE BACK RIVER

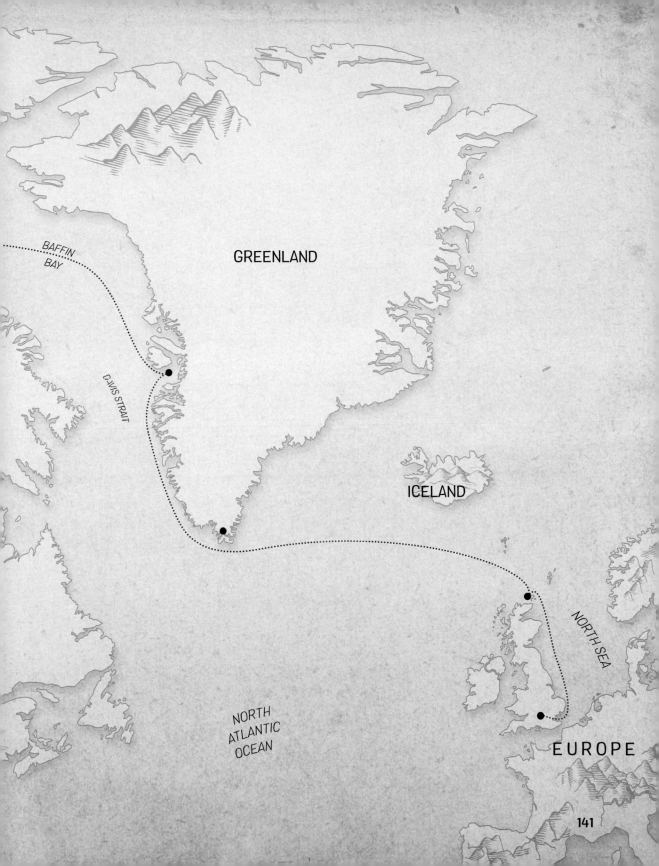

BAFFIN
BAY

GREENLAND

DAVIS STRAIT

ICELAND

NORTH SEA

NORTH
ATLANTIC
OCEAN

EUROPE

YOUR EXPEDITION : Disappeared

September 1848: Montreal Island, Mouth of the Back River

MONTREAL
ISLAND

> "(They were) carrying a number of skulls ... there were more than four ... also bones from legs and arms that appeared to have been sawed off."
>
> — Captain Francis McClintock, reporting Inuit eyewitness accounts of seeing white men

On a low beach of small rounded stones at the water's edge, you squat near a fire crackling from wood that you have torn off one of the sleds. The drifting delicious smell of cooking meat makes you salivate yet torments you.

Your surgeons have removed the muscles from the bodies of the fallen to prepare meals for the survivors — including brain, heart, liver, kidneys and bone marrow — leaving no part wasted.

Your surgeons — with great respect and sadness — have dealt with the bodies of those who have fallen, and all of you accept that if you do not resort to cannibalism, you will not survive. Mercifully beyond sight of the campfire are the remains.

Grim as it sounds, thorough cooking makes it somehow palatable and ensures that what you eat doesn't sicken you or your men.

Difficult as it is to acknowledge how you gained those precious nutrients, they have given you strength again, enough to continue farther south from King William Island.

Sledging over Hummocky Ice, April 1853, from *A Series of Eight Sketches in Colour ... of the Voyage of H.M.S.* Investigator *...*, by Samuel Gurney Cresswell, the first Royal Navy man to cross the Northwest Passage, although he traveled by ship and sledge.

You and your crew move across the ice of the strait to the mainland. Now you are less than 120 km (75 mi.) away from the mouth of the river that will take you to the Hudson's Bay outpost at Great Slave Lake.

To add to this hope is an unexpected sight.

Other humans! A search party sent over land! You are saved!

It is a hope as short-lived as your time with them. These are not Europeans, but Inuit men and women and children in furs, hunting seals out on the ice.

You can tell by their body language that they are reluctant to be among you.

With a flash of insight, you believe you understand. From the point of view of the Inuit, you are a party of roughly 50 men, hairy as monsters, with sunken eyes and protruding cheekbones, carrying guns and knives and hatchets. Worse, appearing as strangers from a featureless horizon, you are carrying what appear to be the body parts of other men. If you were a father or a mother, would you want to endanger your children?

Manellia and Adelik, an Inuit family, from John Ross's *Narrative of a Second Voyage*

When a few of the families provide you and your men with seal meat, is it shared as a gift? Or a fear that you will take their precious resources and, in so doing, deprive their families? Or to distract you from killing them so that they can flee, as they did, at the earliest opportunity?

The seal meat is rich in fat and the nutrients it takes to stave off scurvy. It provides enough energy for you to reach the mainland. But too soon, you and your men are back to the point of starvation again.

Fort Resolution, on the shores of Great Slave Lake, was built in 1819 by the Hudson's Bay Company.

Your body's fat reserves are long gone, and now your body begins to digest its own muscles and then feed on its own organs. This is the inexorable process of autocannibalization — your body has begun to eat itself.

Eventually, you and your men are unable to continue. Another man dies.

Inuit Survival Techniques

Explorer John Rae was famous for his ability to travel long distances in the Arctic, living off the land with little equipment. He was one of the few of his day to recognize that he should learn from those who had spent generations upon generations developing survival techniques in the harshest conditions on the planet. These, of course, were Inuit, skilled at reading weather, wind and ice conditions.

In the summer, Inuit hunted caribou, which roamed in large herds. Not a single part of a slaughtered caribou was wasted. Clothing came from the softer hide of the belly. (It took four caribou to make one parka.) Antlers became tools and tendon converted to thread. Strips of sun-dried meat were saved for winter. Inuit also used the short summer to gather and dry berries, and to catch birds and freshwater fish.

In the winter, Inuit stayed close to the coastline. Their dogs would sniff out the air-holes of seals and Inuit would wait until the seal surfaced and then spear it. Seal hides were waterproof, perfect for shoes and gloves. The meat was nourishing, and the fat high in calories. Blubber was also used as oil for lamps.

Inuit also built shelters — igloos, or *igluit* in Inuktitut — from blocks of snow. They could be connected with tunnels. Heated by blubber oil lamps, they would be comfortably warm inside, even when temperatures outside were -50°C (-60°F).

As for transportation, Inuit traveled light, which of course took far less energy than dragging heavy boats. Their sleds, pulled by dogs, were whalebone structures covered with stretched skins. Kayaks, with whalebone or driftwood frames, used naturally waterproofed stretched sealskins.

As Inuit proved, it was possible to survive and thrive in the Arctic. Explorers who followed their lead did the same. It's one of the reasons that Roald Amundsen and his small crew of six completed the first voyage through the Northwest Passage in 1906.

Inuit girls and women, 1854

No longer are you squeamish about feeding off his remains. But you are in desperate need of more food. It is September, the snow has begun to fall, there are still 100 km (60 mi.) to the mouth of the Back River, then an upstream battle to Fort Resolution at Great Slave Lake. All of you are aware you must travel the river before it freezes.

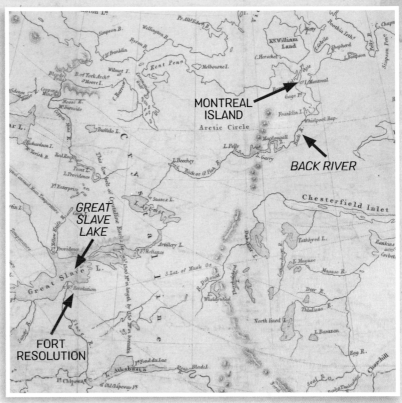

You have grim thoughts. How many more men must die for the survivors to find enough energy to drag the boats to the river? One, two, three?

You find yourself in the dreadful position of hoping for more deaths.

And so it is that more men provide food for the survivors.

Finally, you reach Montreal Island, near the mouth of the Back River, where you can float your boats and begin to ascend the waters to Great Slave Lake. Ahead of you is a bleak landscape of a river with granite shorelines, 83 waterfalls and numerous cascades and rapids.

You leave behind the last evidence of your expedition on Montreal Island. Among the debris that will later be discovered is a can that you had used as a cooking pot. The can was provided by Stephan Goldner, the villain who has enjoyed the last three winters in front of a hearth in his mansion while your men died, likely from the killer he put aboard your ships in those cans of food.

The fate of your men?

You will leave behind evidence of your expedition at Montreal Island, a tiny island in Chantrey Inlet near the mouth of the Back River. Any other traces of your journey have yet to be discovered.

The remains of a pocket chronometer — silver case with an enameled dial — found in an abandoned boat at Erebus Bay, King William Island, by the McClintock search expedition in May 1859

From Montreal Island southward, all traces of your men are lost. More than a century and a half later, historians and scientists will have unearthed no record of what happened. They can only speculate on their fate. Drowned in treacherous rapids? Overcome by the cold of winter? Starvation?

As for you, there will be rumors that for years longer, you lived among those nomadic Inuit.

If so, it will be with the satisfaction that finally your social background did not matter. Instead, you were fully accepted for who you are — for your heart and bravery and resourcefulness.

If so, perhaps you found a companion to love who returned your love, someone to hold you each night and fill your heart with joy, someone to whisper goodbye when you lay down to rest one final time.

You are the man that Inuit called Aglukkaq.

Apply Forensic Techniques to
Solve the Mystery

It was a hot day in the summer of 1971, when, at home in Bedford Village, New York, Samuel Cochran Jr., 61, and his wife, Grace, 63, decided to have some chilled soup straight from the can. It was not a lazy decision. The Bon Vivant can contained vichyssoise, a thick French soup of potatoes and leeks typically served cold.

It tasted spoiled, so after their first spoonfuls they set the soup aside. By then, however, it was too late.

The next morning, Samuel Cochran had double vision and began to have trouble speaking. Both went to the hospital. Samuel died shortly after, and Grace suffered three months of paralysis before recovering.

The obvious culprit was the soup, which was sent to a state health laboratory for testing. A mouse was injected with the soup and it died within 24 hours.

Immediately came the state-wide emergency alert, warning people to be aware of symptoms like vomiting, dizziness, weakness, headache and visual difficulties from dilation of the pupils.

At the same time, an urgent recall began for all 6444 cans of lot number v-141-USA-71 of the vichyssoise produced by Bon Vivant.

What modern forensic knowledge allows you to come to a conclusion about the probable culprit behind this couple's tragedy?

Answer at end of the chapter.

THE SEARCH THEN : 138 Words

Francis Leopold McClintock,
July 1857: Aberdeen, Scotland

Twelve years after the ships disappeared, Lady Franklin was unable to convince government officials to fund yet another search for her husband. But the mystery still had enough fascination that when she appealed to the public for donations to make one last attempt to learn the fate of her husband's expedition, she was able to successfully fund a private expedition.

This was led by Francis Leopold McClintock, who sailed from Aberdeen on July 1, 1857, in a three-masted steam schooner, the *Fox*.

McClintock, like most explorers, was soon frustrated by the ice pack. In September, the *Fox* became stuck for the next eight months; it took them until August 1858 just to reach Beechey Island.

Sir Francis Leopold McClintock

The *Fox on a Rock Near Buchan Island*, from McClintock's *The Voyage of the "Fox" in the Arctic Seas*, 1859.

147

The following summer, progress was so grim they barely made it another 160 km (100 mi.) south, where the ships were stuck again for a second time. Here, McClintock met Inuit who told him that a ship had been crushed by ice and, although the crew had landed safely on King William Island, some white people had starved to death.

He needed to search the island. *Were there still survivors?*

Finally, in April 1859, McClintock was able to send out sledge parties from the *Fox* onto King William Island.

Captain McClintock's First Interview with the Esquimaux at Cape Victoria shows the explorer getting a warm welcome from the Inuit he met. From the Illustrated London News, October 1859.

Lieutenant William Hobson led one party. Reaching a high point at the northwest shoreline, he sat down to rest. Surveying the scene, he blinked in disbelief. Below, on the flat gravel appeared to be a rock as tall as a man. He peered through a naval telescope and realized it was a stone cairn. The closer look also showed heaps of discarded clothing and blankets and mattresses. Astounded, he rushed over and saw more evidence that could have been left behind only by officers and crew of the Franklin expedition — four iron stoves, kettles and pans, rusted meat tins, shovels, saws and much more.

He'd discovered where the officers and crew had made landfall after abandoning ship.

Discovery of the Franklin Expedition Boat on King William's Land by Lieutenant Hobson

Inside the cairn was a letter dated May 28, 1847, with notes written on the margins in April 1848. All the years of searching had resulted in the discovery of the only written record left by the expedition — its meager 138 words.

From it, the world would learn that the *Erebus* and *Terror* had first wintered near Beechey Island. And the date of Sir John Franklin's death. It also said that Crozier had decided to abandon ships north and west of King William Island in April 1848 and begin a trek southward. (This note did have a notably significant error, giving the date of the expedition's winter camp at Beechey Island as 1846 to 1847 instead of 1845 to 1846.)

At the western edge of the island, Hobson also discovered a boat from one of the ships. It contained relics of the expedition, as well as skeletons of two crew members. Puzzling to him — and future historians — were the contents of the boat. It included all sorts of items useless for survival, such as silk handkerchiefs, scented soap, slippers, combs and many, many books. Inexplicably, the boat was facing north, in a direction opposite to where Crozier had written the men were headed.

McClintock also found a human skeleton on the southern coast, still clothed. Although a seaman's certificate with the name Chief Petty Officer Henry Peglar was found on the body, the uniform on the skeleton belonged to a ship's steward, who was probably carrying the papers for Peglar.

Like John Rae in 1854, McClintock met Inuit who possessed items from the Franklin expedition, including a knife, telescope case and silver spoons and forks bearing the initials of Franklin and of Crozier.

And like Rae before him, McClintock also heard Inuit stories about the survivors. Inuit had found the wreck of an empty deserted ship forced ashore by ice. To his dismay, he learned that books, most likely among them the captain's logs, had been playthings for Inuit children until destroyed by weather.

As the discoverer of the lost expedition's fate, he returned to England in September of that year as a hero. He received a knighthood and a huge monetary reward, then wrote a book about it: *The Voyage of the "Fox" in the Arctic Seas: A Narrative of the Discovery of the Fate of Sir John Franklin and His Companions.*

"Anything that Inuit are not accustomed to, they have no use for them, a box or material they can use, they keep them, but the content is thrown away or broken up, as they are too heavy for them to take with them, as they are continously on the move, all the time."

— Simon Okpakok

Map drawn by Oonalee, Netsilingmiut man, in 1859, showing the location where he told Captain F. L. McClintock one of Franklin's ships had sunk off Kiikertaksuak (King William Island)

149

The Sir John Franklin Expedition Memorial, Royal Naval College in Greenwich, in London, England

Much to the satisfaction of Lady Franklin, on the evidence of the letter found in the cairn, McClintock had proven that her husband had died before the ships were abandoned, and before any officers and crew turned to cannibalism to survive.

Instead of appearing as a villain or a failure, Sir John Franklin would be honored as a man who sacrificed his life to help discover the Northwest Passage.

As for Franklin's niece, Sophy Cracroft?

After Lady Franklin's death in 1875, Sophy spent the final years of her life devoted to collecting and organizing Lady Franklin's almost 2000 letters and 200 journals, eventually going blind and dying before her task was completed. She never married.

Before she went blind, each time Sophy saw any mention of Francis Rawdon Moira Crozier in Lady Franklin's correspondences, her thoughts could well have wandered to what might have been.

After all, when Sir Leopold McClintock once asked Lady Franklin about Sophy's true feelings toward Francis Crozier, her reply was simple yet revealing: "The pity is, Sir Leopold, Sophy liked the man, but not the sailor."

Only known photo of Sophy Cracroft (center) and Lady Franklin, with guides in Yosemite Valley. Detail of a stereograph. Courtesy of the George Eastman Museum.

There it was. The paradox that ensured Crozier's heartbreak. When Crozier first proposed to her, after 35 years of wandering the world to serve the Royal Navy, he had no permanent home. Perhaps Crozier felt his only hope of winning her had been to gain glory, promotion and wealth from a successful passage through the Arctic. Yet Sophy, as noted in her journals, was not interested in becoming the wife of a commander who would be gone for years.

Perhaps in her final years, however, she did regret her decision, as hinted at in a letter she had written years earlier to Franklin, sent along in the 1850s on one of the ships tasked to search for the expedition.

At the bottom of the letter, with proper Victorian discretion that spoke far louder than the words she penned, she had added one last sentence: *Pray remember me very kindly to Captain Crozier.*

The letter returned to her unopened.

Elsewhere at the time ...

A Free-Falling Safety Demonstration

Francis Leopold McClintock launched his search for the fate of the *Erebus* and *Terror* in a year when the first photo studio was opened and when the rules of baseball changed to make nine innings a game.

The year 1857 was also the year that an inventor named Elisha Graves Otis was about to transform city skylines — he installed an elevator in a five-story department store in New York.

An elevator free-fall safety demonstration in 1853

What made the elevator the first of its kind were the safety brakes he demonstrated in what appeared to be a death-defying act at the nearby World's Fair in 1853. Standing high above the ground on a platform held in place between two columns by a single rope, Otis invited someone with an ax to chop the single rope. Instead of plummeting to the ground, the platform — Otis with it — fell only a couple of inches before brakes locked it into place.

With people now willing to trust the safety of elevators, buildings grew higher and higher. Before the Otis Elevator, the highest floors of a building were undesirable because of the effort to climb the stairs. After, the penthouse view was what everyone wanted.

OF SHIPS AND MEN : Aglukkaq

Francis Rawdon Moira Crozier,
1858 to present time: Baker Lake, Nunavut

Amundsen's route through the Northwest Passage is marked in pink. Franklin's route is blue. Under different circumstances, the Franklin expedition might have succeeded in being first to sail the passage.

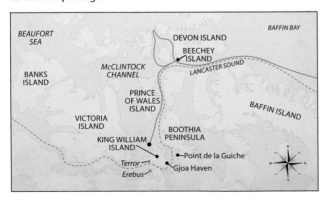

Charles Francis Hall and Lieutenant Frederick Gustavus Schwatka were not the only Arctic searchers to hear stories told by Inuit about the ghost ships.

In 1903, Roald Amundsen, a Norwegian, became the first explorer to successfully navigate the Northwest Passage by sea. He met Inuit who told him that they had found a deserted ship, entered it and eaten some of the tinned meat inside. Some became ill. Others died.

If true, decades after Stephan Goldner had vanished to escape bankruptcy, his grim legacy of spoiled food prevailed.

The illness and deaths of those unsuspecting Inuit point to colonies of *Clostridium botulinum*, a bacterium that produces the most potent toxin known to mankind.

Symptoms of those afflicted by botulism? Blurred or double vision. Nausea, vomiting, abdominal cramps. Diarrhea. Muscle weakness. Paralysis that begins with the face and moves to the limbs.

Those in favor of declaring botulism the answer to the medical mystery of Franklin's expedition remind us that a parliamentary inquiry proved that Stephan Goldner produced tinned food in conditions that could have introduced the deadly bacterium into the food.

One argument against naming botulism as the main culprit is that Goldner used the same methods to supply canned food to other ships, including ships sent to search for the *Erebus* and *Terror*, but there is no recorded evidence that they suffered outbreaks of poisoning by botulism.

This argument, though, ignores the circumstance of the ever-dwindling supply of coal on the *Erebus* and *Terror*.

To destroy any toxins in it, food needs to be heated to more than 85°C (185°F) for at least five minutes. If we presume that the canned food on the other ships was consistently cooked at a sufficiently high temperature for at least five minutes, those sailors would have consumed the contents safely.

On the other hand, as the coal supplies of the *Erebus* and *Terror* diminished, two and three years into the expedition, it's easy to envision that Franklin's remaining officers and crew ate the food cold and uncooked, thus taking the botulism toxin directly into their weakened bodies. The same fate would have befallen Inuit who found the food and consumed it uncooked, as in the stories told to Amundsen.

This would also explain the death of First Lieutenant Graham Gore, assuming he had departed for King William Island as a healthy man, supplied with cans of food to sustain him for the arduous round trip over ice. With no fuel for fires to heat the cans, it is not unreasonable to speculate that he would have eaten uncooked contaminated food and could have been botulism's first victim.

Forensic techniques add one more indicator of the likelihood of botulism as the main killer. Owen Beattie's autopsy of William Braine on Beechey Island did show the existence of the *Clostridium* bacterium in the sailor's exhumed body.

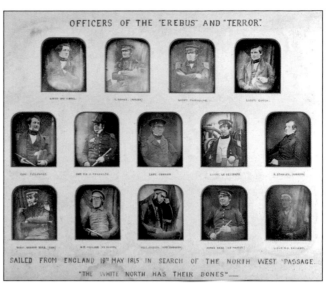

OFFICERS OF THE "EREBUS" AND "TERROR."

SAILED FROM ENGLAND 19ᵗʰ MAY 1845 IN SEARCH OF THE NORTH WEST PASSAGE.
"THE WHITE NORTH HAS THEIR BONES"

Lady Franklin commissioned these portraits of the officers of the expedition.

Douglas Stenton excavating the grave at NgLj-3 that contained the remains of three members of the Franklin expedition, including Warrant Officer John Gregory of HMS *Erebus*. In 2021, Stenton and other scientists matched DNA from tooth and bone samples from this site on King William Island to DNA from a living descendant of Gregory. It was the first positive identification of a Franklin crew member's remains.

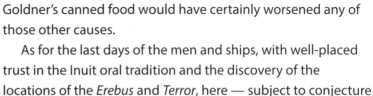

At the very least, what has been suggested by forensics is that officers and crew died from a combination of scurvy, pneumonia and tuberculosis. Any sickness caused by

Man Proposes, God Disposes, by Sir Edwin Landseer, imagines a scene in which polar bears attack the remains of members of Franklin's expedition. The painting captured popular attention, but Lady Franklin found it offensive, and students at the university where it now hangs believe it to be haunted.

Goldner's canned food would have certainly worsened any of those other causes.

As for the last days of the men and ships, with well-placed trust in the Inuit oral tradition and the discovery of the locations of the *Erebus* and *Terror*, here — subject to conjecture and debate — is a reasonable reconstruction of events:

In April 1848, Francis Crozier, along with fellow captain James Fitzjames, abandoned the ships. They led all the remaining men, with three sledges of supplies and some of the ships' boats, to south of Victory Point on King William Island, where they left a note in a cairn.

To lighten their load, they left behind many supplies, later found by Lieutenant William Robert Hobson.

They began to march southward, intending to reach the Back River, hoping to travel upriver to the Hudson's Bay post at Great Slave Lake. Many simply died as they walked, leaving behind a line of bones to be found decades later.

After about 80 km (50 mi.), the party split in two, leaving behind the boats. It is believed that those unable to travel were given instructions to return to Victory Point to wait for rescue, and as a result, the boats they left behind were pointing north.

Some of the survivors managed to return to the ships, which were later released in a thaw and either drifted south with the currents or were manned by surviving crew.

Francis Crozier, known as Aglukkaq — "He Who Takes Long Strides"

Inuit had contact with these outsiders, with descriptions passing from one generation to the next. More than one story told of a meeting with the man they called Aglukkaq, the same name that Francis Crozier had been given by Inuit in his first dealings with them on an earlier expedition.

Four survivors and a dog were seen over the next few years after this first contact. Again, one of them was named Aglukkaq.

There is no certainty, however, that the Aglukkaq of these Inuit stories was the same man in all situations or if he even was Francis Crozier, since the name "He Who Takes Long Strides" could have easily been given to another outsider.

However, if this indeed was Crozier, there is one last and tantalizing speculation about his final fate, based on unverified Inuit reports collected between 1852 and 1858. According to them, Crozier and one other expedition member were seen in the Baker Lake area, about 400 km (250 mi.) to the south.

Parks Canada's support barge *Qiniqtirjuaq* with members of the Underwater Archaeology Team positioned above the wreck of HMS *Erebus* in summer 2019. Future archaeological work is sure to reveal much more about the the fate of the expedition.

It was farther south, at Angikuni Lake, in 1948, that Farley Mowat, a Canadian writer and early environmentalist, discovered an ancient cairn. It was not of Inuit construction. Inside were shreds of a hardwood box with dovetail joints — a common European construction technique not used by Inuit.

Flimsy evidence perhaps, but it does allow for the romantic notion — for those who want to believe — that Francis Rawdon Moira Crozier spent his last years among a people who welcomed him as the explorer he was.

Mystery SOLVED

Congratulations if you realized the similarity between Samuel Cochran Jr.'s death and the way that many of the officers and crew could have died on the *Terror* and *Erebus* — by eating unheated tinned food that had been contaminated by the bacterium *Clostridium*.

It was the botulism toxin, then, that became the deadly poison.

In the case of Bon Vivant — as with Stephan Goldner and his tinned food for the Admiralty over a century earlier — it was determined that the company had undercooked the food and sealed it in the cans.

As a result, Bon Vivant was forced to destroy its entire stock of canned food and subsequently declared bankruptcy.

Recommended Resources

It was a wonderful adventure researching the lost Franklin expedition through a great variety of books, magazines and website sources. From all of those, here is a list of essential resources for kids, parents and teachers who would like to learn more. Of particular note are the sources that you can find at www.canadianmysteries.ca, where you'll also learn about other great unsolved mysteries in Canadian history.

BOOKS, JOURNALS AND MAGAZINES

Battersby, William. *James Fitzjames: The Mystery Man of the Franklin Expedition*. Toronto: Dundurn, 2010.

Beattie, Owen, and John Geiger. *Frozen in Time: The Fate of the Franklin Expedition*. Vancouver: Greystone Books, 2017.

Bown, Stephen R. *Scurvy: How a Surgeon, a Mariner, and a Gentleman Solved the Greatest Medical Mystery of the Age of Sail*. Markham, Ontario: Thomas Allen Publishers, 2003.

Charles River Editors. *Captain John Franklin's Lost Expedition: The History of the British Explorer's Arctic Voyage in Search of the Northwest Passage*. Ann Arbor, MI: Charles River Editors, 2016.

Cookman, Scott. *Ice Blink: The Tragic Fate of Sir John Franklin's Lost Polar Expedition*. Hoboken, NJ: Wiley Press, 2008.

Geiger, John, and Alanna Mitchell. *Franklin's Lost Ship: The Historic Discovery of HMS* Erebus. Toronto: HarperCollins Publishers, 2015.

Horowitz, B. Zane. "Polar Poisons: Did Botulism Doom the Franklin Expedition?" *Journal of Toxicology: Clinical Toxicology* 41, no. 6 (October 30, 2003): 841–847 (www.tandfonline.com/doi/abs/10.1081/CLT-120025349).

Hutchinson, Gillian. *Sir John Franklin's* Erebus *and* Terror *Expedition: Lost and Found*. London: Adlard Coles Nautical, 2017.

Latta, Jeffrey Blair. *The Franklin Conspiracy: An Astonishing Solution to the Lost Arctic Expedition*. Toronto: Dundurn, 2001.

Long, Kat. "19 Facts About the Franklin Expedition, the Real-Life Inspiration for *The Terror*." *Mental Floss*, April 26, 2018 (www.mentalfloss.com/article/537632/facts-about-the-franklin-expedition-the-terror).

Mays, S., George Maat and Hans H. De Boer. "Scurvy as a Factor in the Loss of the 1845 Franklin Expedition to the Arctic: A Reconsideration." *International Journal of Osteoarchaeology* 25, no. 3 (February 2013): 334–344 (www.researchgate.net/publication/264667589_Scurvy_as_a_factor_in_the_loss_of_the_1845_Franklin_expedition_to_the_Arctic_a_reconsideration).

Moneo, Shannon. "Victoria Entrepreneur Unlocks Health Mysteries Through Hair Analysis." *Douglas Magazine*, July 31, 2017 (www.douglasmagazine.com/victoria-entrepreneur-unlocks-health-mysteries-hair-analysis/).

"Navigating Constitution." *The Captain Speaks*. Captain's Clerk, 2011 (www.captainsclerk.info/speaks/book18.html).

Palin, Michael. *Erebus: One Ship, Two Epic Voyages, and the Greatest Naval Mystery of All Time*. Vancouver: Greystone Books, 2019.

Potter, Russell A. *Finding Franklin: The Untold Story of a 165-Year Search*. Montreal: McGill-Queen's University Press, 2016.

Rodgers, Garry. "Forensic Facts From the Fatal Franklin Expedition." *HuffPost*, January 19, 2017 (www.huffpost.com/entry/franklin-expedition-northwest-passage_b_9013366).

Roobol, John. *Franklin's Fate: An Investigation Into What Happened to the Lost 1845 Expedition of Sir John Franklin*. Canterbury: The Conrad Press, 2019.

Rowbothman, Sheila. "Canned Food Sealed Icemen's Fate." *History Today*, October 10, 1987 (www.historytoday.com/archive/canned-food-sealed-icemens-fate).

Smith, Kiona N. "Strands of Hair Shed Light on Doomed 19th-Century Arctic Expedition." *Ars Technica*, September 30, 2018 (www.arstechnica.com/science/2018/09/did-lead-poisoning-finish-off-a-doomed-arctic-expedition/).

Smith, Michael. *Captain Francis Crozier: Last Man Standing?* Cork, Ireland: Collins Press, 2006.

Solly, Meilan. "Lead Poisoning Wasn't a Major Factor in the Mysterious Demise of the Franklin Expedition." *Smithsonian Magazine*, August 28, 2018 (www.smithsonianmag.com/smart-news/lead-poisoning-wasnt-major-factor-mysterious-demise-franklin-expedition-180970150/).

Watson, Paul. *Ice Ghosts: The Epic Hunt for the Lost Franklin Expedition*. New York City: W.W. Norton, 2017.

Williams, Martin. "British Ship from 1845 Franklin Expedition Found by Canada." *The Guardian*, September 10, 2014 (www.theguardian.com/world/2014/sep/09/british-ship-1845-franklin-expedition-found-canada).

Wilson, John. "Did Botulism Fell Franklin's Crew?" *Globe and Mail*, March 25, 2000 (www.theglobeandmail.com/arts/did-botulism-fell-franklins-crew/article766779/).

WEBSITES

Building HMS Terror: A blog by Matthew Betts, a model builder who served as a historical advisor for AMC's series *The Terror*. See http://buildingterror .blogspot.com.

Canadian Geographic: See www.canadiangeographic.ca /topic/franklin-expedition. Canadian Geographic Education also offers lesson plans about the expedition in the traditional language of Inuktitut!

Erebus and Terror Files: A blog by engineer and Franklin expedition enthusiast Peter Carney, at www.erebusandterrorfiles.blogspot.com.

Great Unsolved Mysteries in Canadian History: See www.canadianmysteries.ca, especially *The Franklin Mystery: Life & Death in the Arctic* at www.canadianmysteries.ca/sites/franklin/home /homeIntro_en.htm.

History Archive: See www.historyarchive.org for links to historic books, illustrations and maps. Search for the terms "Arctic," "Exploration," "Franklin" and "Terror and Erebus."

Linda Hall Library: *Ice: A Victorian Romance* is an exhibition of 55 rare books and journals, first displayed at the Linda Hall Library in 2008. See them at https://ice .lindahall.org.

Parks Canada: You can learn more about the Wrecks of HMS *Erebus* and HMS *Terror* National Historic Site, co-managed by Inuit and Parks Canada, here: www.pc.gc.ca/en/lhn-nhs/nu/epaveswrecks.

Royal Museums Greenwich: Visit www.collections.rmg .co.uk/collections.html to see original Franklin expedition relics, maps, polar equipment, ship plans and more. If you are ever in London, England, be sure to visit the National Maritime Museum Greenwich.

The Search for the Northwest Passage: A British Library page about Captain James Cook that features Arctic explorers. Go to www.bl.uk/the-voyages-of-captain -james-cook/themes/the-search-for-the-northwest -passage.

Visions of the North: A blog by author and historian Russell Potter. Go to www.visionsnorth.blogspot.com.

Acknowledgments

Special thanks to Gjoa Haven Inuit elder and interpreter Simon Okpakok. Your contributions and careful review of the manuscript have been invaluable and are greatly appreciated. Equally heartfelt thanks to Lyle Dick, public historian and co-creator of the Franklin Mystery website, and to Jonathan Moore of Parks Canada, for reviewing the manuscript and making invaluable suggestions. Any errors in this book, however, are my own!

Kathleen Fraser, thank you! While your official description in this project is editor, I have no doubt that you are one of the all-time great sleuths of Canadian history. Along with your insights and suggestions in regard to the manuscript, again and again you found gems of stories that elevated the final book to what it is.

Barb Kelly, your artistry in blending photographs, illustrations and maps with design elements transformed the black-and-white lines of manuscript into a vibrant presentation of the unfolding mystery, making it a pleasure to the eyes. Thank you so very much!

Index

The letters carved in the handle of this knife identify it as belonging to Cornelius Hickey, Caulker's Mate, of HMS *Terror*.

Photos and Illustrations

We are grateful to the individuals and organizations that granted permission to reproduce their images in this book. They are credited below.

Many of the historic images and artworks included here can be found in books that are now in the public domain. We have tried to ascertain copyright for all images. Historian Lyle Dick, research director for The Franklin Mystery project, was helpful in guiding us to the sources of images reproduced at that website. (See the Archives at www.canadianmysteries.ca/sites/franklin/.) Where possible, we have noted original sources here or in photo captions.

The maps that open each expedition, plus maps on pages 9, 17, 59, 72, 77, 81, 102, 107, 131, 136 and 152, were created or adapted from existing maps by book designer Barb Kelly.

Front cover: *The Crew of HMS Terror Saving the Boats and Provisions on the Night of 15th March (1837)*, 1838, by George Hyde Chambers. Collection of the Beaverbrook Art Gallery, 1981.04.

Back cover: Detail from *HMS* Erebus *and HMS* Terror, by J. Franklin Wright; Lieutenant Irving's grave (see page 81); Douglas Stenton at NgLj-3 (see page 153).

Endpapers: *Discoveries of Captains Ross, Parry and Franklin in the Arctic Regions in 1818, 1819, 1820, 1821 and 1822* (see page 26).

Page 1: Detail from *HMS* Erebus *and* Terror *in the Antarctic*, by John Wilson Carmichael. National Maritime Museum, Greenwich, London, Caird Fund.

Pages 2–3: Officers of the Franklin Expedition, photographs from a mounted set of daguerreotype portraits made by Richard Beard in May 1845 (D8760/F/LIB/8/1/5). Courtesy of Derbyshire Record Office. (Originals from which the Derbyshire copies were made are at the Scott Polar Research Institute.)

Page 4: *HMS* Erebus *in the Ice, 1846*, by François Etienne Musin. National Maritime Museum, Greenwich, London, Caird Collection.

Episode One: Heroes Depart

Page 8: Captain Francis Crozier. From the 1845 daguerreotype by Richard Beard.

Page 9: [**Top**] Map of Antarctic routes Crozier and James Clark Ross travelled. Mapswire / Barb Kelly. [**Bottom**] Detail from *Commander James Clark Ross*, by John Robert Wildman. National Maritime Museum, Greenwich, London, Caird Fund.

Page 10: Erebus *and the* Terror *in New Zealand, August 1841*, by John Wilson Carmichael. National Maritime Museum, Greenwich, London, Caird Fund.

Page 11: Captain Sir John Franklin, National Archives of Canada/C-001352, from *A Narrative of a Second Expedition to the Shores of the Polar Sea in the Years 1825, 1826, and 1827* by John Franklin (Philadelphia: Carey, Lea and Carey, 1828).

Page 12: Steam tug towing a ship. iStock.com/duncan1980.

Page 13: [**Left**] *Sir William Edward Parry*, by Samuel William Reynolds, published by and after William Haines, 1827. © National Portrait Gallery, London. [**Center**] *Sir George Back*, by Edward Francis Finden, published by John Samuel Murray, after Richard Woodman, 1828. © National Portrait Gallery, London. [**Right**] *Sir John Ross*, by Richard James Lane, printed by Jérémie Graf, published by Joseph Dickinson, after Benjamin Rawlinson Faulkner, 1834. © National Portrait Gallery, London.

Page 14: Collision of *Erebus* and *Terror* in Antarctic waters. From *A Voyage of Discovery and Research in the Southern and Antarctic Regions, During the Years 1839–43* (Vol. 2, Frontispiece), by James Clark Ross (London: John Murray, 1847).

Page 15: *Map Shewing the Discoveries made by British Officers in the Arctic regions, from the Year 1818 to 1826*, from *A Narrative of a Second Expedition to the Shores of the Polar Sea …*, by John Franklin (London: 1828). Courtesy of the John Carter Brown Library.

Page 16: *Summer Tents of the Esquimaux, Igloolik*, from *Journal of a Second Voyage for the Discovery of a North-West Passage*, by William Edward Parry (1824). Courtesy of the John Carter Brown Library.

Page 17: [**Top**] Barb Kelly / base map by FreeVectorMaps.com, https://freevectormaps.com. [**Bottom**] Louie Kamookak at Peabody Point. Photo by Jason Fulford.

Page 18: [**Top**] Relics of the Franklin Expedition, ca. 1845. Library and Archives Canada / W.H. Coverdale collection of Canadiana Manoir Richelieu Collection / e010958396. From *A Series of Fourteen Sketches, Made During the Voyage up Wellington Channel in Search of Sir John Franklin, K.C.H., and the Missing Crews of H.M. Discovery-Ships* Erebus *and* Terror: *Together with a Short Account of Each Drawing*, by Walter William May (London: Day and Son, 1855) [**Bottom**] *Neptune, the property of W.E. Gosling Esqr*, from *Engravings of Lions, Tigers, Panthers, Leopards, Dogs, &c., Chiefly after the Designs of Sir Edwin Landseer by his Brother Thomas Landseer*. Courtesy of New York Public Library Digital Collections.

Page 19: [**Top**] Record case found by W. R. Hobson of the McClintock Expedition. National Maritime Museum, Greenwich, London. [**Bottom**] Bog body Tollund Man. Courtesy of Nationalmuseet, Denmark.

Episode Two: Smooth Sailing

Page 22: *Island of Disco and Icebergs*, from *A Voyage of Discovery, Made under the Orders of the Admiralty, in His Majesty's Ships* Isabella *and* Alexander, *for the Purpose of Exploring Baffin's Bay, and Inquiring into the Probability of a North-West Passage* (London: John Murray, 1819). Courtesy of the John Carter Brown Library.

Page 23: [**Top**] *Danish Whaling Station*, by Abraham Speeck, 1634.

Page 24: Cutaway view of HMS *Erebus*. GRAPHIC NEWS.

Page 25: Sir John Franklin. From the 1845 daguerreotype by Richard Beard.

Page 26: [**Top**] *The Fury Grounded on Fury Beach*, from William Edward Parry's *Journal of a Third Voyage*, 1826. Courtesy of The Linda Hall Library of Science, Engineering & Technology. [**Bottom**] Map detail from *Discoveries of Captains Ross, Parry and Franklin in the Arctic Regions in 1818, 1819, 1820, 1821 and 1822*. N.d. Mccormick_142 Andrew McCormick Maps and Prints. University of British Columbia Library Rare Books and Special Collections.

Page 27: *Terror* trapped by ice near Southhampton. From *Narrative of an Expedition in HMS* Terror, *Undertaken with a View to Geographical Discovery on the Arctic Shores, in the Years 1836–37*, by George Back (London: John Murray, 1838). Courtesy of Toronto Public Library.

Page 28: [**Top**] Franklin's cabin in the *Erebus*. From the *Illustrated London News*, May 24, 1845. [**Bottom**] Mammoths. Detail from a mural by Charles R. Knight.

Page 30: [**Top**] *The Dolphin squeezed by ice, with the Union looking on* (detail), from John Franklin's *Narrative of a Second Expedition …*, 1828. Courtesy of the John Carter Brown Library. [**Bottom**] Seaboot. National Maritime Museum, Greenwich, London.

Page 31: Macquarie Harbour settlement, Van Dieman's Land, 1833, by William Buelow Gould. Courtesy of the Mitchell Library, State Library of New South Wales.

Page 32: Lockstitch sewing machine. From *Great Inventors and Their Inventions*, by Frank Puterbaugh Bachman (American Book Co., 1918).

Page 33: Owen Beattie. Photo by Laura Stanley, courtesy of Canadian Geographic.

Page 34: [Top] Hall with Inuit. From Charles Francis Hall's *Arctic researches, and life among the Esquimaux* (Harper & Brothers, 1865). Image from the Biodiversity Heritage Library. [Middle] Inuit sledge. From the *Narrative of the Second Arctic Expedition made by Charles F. Hall: His Voyage to Repulse Bay, Sledge Journeys to the Straits of Fury and Hecla and to King William's Land, and Residence among the Eskimos, during the Years 1864-'69*, edited under the orders of the Hon. Secretary of the Navy, by J. E. Nourse. Image from the Biodiversity Heritage Library.

Page 35: Skulls of members of the Franklin expedition discovered and buried by William Skinner and Paddy Gibson, King William Island, N.W.T. Library and Archives Canada/Dudley Copland fonds/a147732.

Episode Three: Arktos

Page 38: Dip circle found near Ross Cairn, Victory Point. National Maritime Museum, Greenwich, London.

Page 39: [Top] James Fitzjames. From the 1845 daguerreotype by Richard Beard. [Middle] Sketch of magnetic station by Fitzjames. National Archives, Kew, United Kingdom. Records of the Meteorological Office, BJ3 17 (2), letter of James Fitzjames to Edward Sabine, June 3, 1845 / *The Franklin Mystery: Life and Death in the Arctic* (www.canadianmysteries.ca). [Bottom] Interior of magnetic observatory. From *The Voyage of the "Fox" in the Arctic Seas: A Narrative of the Discovery of the Fate of Sir John Franklin and His Companions*, by Francis Leopold McClintock (London: 1859). © British Library Board (10460.d.2).

Page 40: [Top] Crow's nest. Walter and Arthur Wellman Collection, National Air and Space Museum, Smithsonian Institution. [Bottom] Detail of map from John Barrow's *Voyages of Discovery …, 1846*. Courtesy of The Linda Hall Library of Science, Engineering & Technology.

Page 41: The paddler at sea on board his boat cloak. *Boat-Cloak, or Cloak-Boat, constructed of Macintosh India Rubber cloth, with Paddle, Umbrella, Sail, Bellows, etc. Invented by P. H.* © British Library Board (1269.d.5).

Page 42: Chip log. Science History Images / Alamy Stock Photo.

Page 43: The *Gjøa*, from Roald Amundsen's *The North West Passage, 1903–1907*.

Page 44: *The Crews of HMS* Hecla & Griper *cutting into Winter Harbour*. From William Parry's *Journal of a Second Voyage for the Discovery of a North-West Passage* (1821). Courtesy of the John Carter Brown Library.

Page 45: [Top] Beechey Island winter quarters. © British Library Board (10460.d.5). [Bottom] Fury and Hecla at Igloolik. *Journal of a Second Voyage for the Discovery of a North-West Passage from the Atlantic to the Pacific; Performed in the Years 1821-22-23, in His Majesty's Ships* Fury and Hecla, *under the orders of William Edward Parry*. John Murray, Publisher to the Admiralty, and Board of Longitude (1824). JCB Archive of Early American Images. Courtesy of the John Carter Brown Library.

Page 47: [Top] Sir John Barrow, attributed to John Jackson, 1818. © National Portrait Gallery, London. [Bottom] Detail of a map of the polar regions by August Heinrich Petermann. Admiralty, *Further Correspondence and Proceedings*, 1852. Courtesy of The Linda Hall Library of Science, Engineering & Technology.

Page 48: Rescue of John Ross and crew of *Victory* by *Isabella*. Engraving by Edward Francis Finden for John Tallis & Co. National Maritime Museum, Greenwich, London.

Page 49: Aerial wheel. Photo by Tom Heavey, used with permission of Irish Vintage Scene Publishing Ltd.

Page 50: Gjoa Haven, 2019. Photo by Kerry Raymond.

Page 51: Ipirvik (Ebierbing), 1879. From the *Narrative of the Second Arctic Expedition Made by Charles F. Hall …*, edited under the orders of the Hon. Secretary of the Navy, by J. E. Nourse. Image from the Biodiversity Heritage Library.

Page 52: [Top] Louie Kamookak. Photo by Jason Fulford. [Bottom] Beechey Island's harbor. Photo by LawrieM.

Page 53: [Top] Sketch map of King William Land provided by In-nook-poo-zhee-jook to Charles Francis Hall, 1869. From *Narrative of the Second Arctic Expedition Made by Charles F. Hall …*, edited under the orders of the Hon. Secretary of the Navy, by J. E. Nourse. Image from the Biodiversity Heritage Library. [Middle] Ross and Inuit. From *Narrative of a Second Voyage in Search of a North-West Passage, and of a Residence in the Arctic Regions During the Years 1829, 1830, 1831, 1832, 1833*, by John Ross (1835). Alamy.

Episode Four: Endless Night

Page 56: Rat leaving a ship. Drawing by A.L. Tarter, 194- Wellcome Collection (CC BY 4.0).

Page 57: [Top] Coal mining. Illustration from *The White Slaves of England* (1853). [Bottom] Preston's Patent Illuminator. From *The Repertory of Arts, Manufactures, and Agriculture*, Volume XXXII, Second Series (1818).

Page 58: Frederic Edwin Church, *The Icebergs*, 1861. Oil on canvas, 64½ x 112½ in. (1 m 63.83 cm x 2 m 85.751 cm). Dallas Museum of Art, gift of Norma and Lamar Hunt. 1979.28. Image courtesy of Dallas Museum of Art.

Page 60: Graves on Beechey Island. Engraving by James Hamilton, based on a sketch by Elisha Kent Kane. From *The U.S. Grinnell Expedition in Search of Sir John Franklin*, by Elisha K. Kane (1854). Wellcome Collection. Public Domain Mark.

Page 61: Portrait of Isaac Newton. Attributed to "English School" (c 1715–1720) by Bonhams.

Page 62: Sir John Ross. Photograph by Maull & Polyblank. Wellcome Collection (CC BY 4.0).

Page 63: [Middle] John Ross's signature, from a later letter to the Admiralty on the advisability of an Arctic Relief Expedition, January 27, 1847. National Archives, Kew, United Kingdom. Admiralty 7/187, Documents relating to Arctic Expeditions. Image from *The Franklin Mystery: Life and Death in the Arctic* (www.canadianmysteries.ca). [Bottom] Replica of Letheon Morton inhaler. Wood Library-Museum of Anesthesiology.

Page 64: Headboards of graves at Beechey. Courtesy of Paul Ward (www.coolantarctica.com).

Page 65: *Beechey Island Site of Sr J. Franklin's Winter Quarters 1845–1846* (1852). University of Manitoba Archives & Special Collections.

Page 66: [Top] John Torrington and [Bottom] John Hartnell. Photos by Brian Spenceley, courtesy of his family.

Page 67: Discarded tins on Beechey Island. Courtesy of Paul Ward (www.coolantarctica.com).

Episode Five: Fateful Decisions

Page 70: *Terror* anchored near iceberg. Painting by Sir George Back. Balfore Archive Images, Alamy.

Page 71: *Eight different specimen of seals sitting on ice floes in the Arctic sea*. Colored etching by J. Bower after J. Stewart. Wellcome Collection (CC BY 4.0).

Page 73: [Top] MV *Nunavik*. Photo by Tim Keane. [Bottom] Grolar bear (*Pizzlies in Osnabrück*) by Corradox (CC BY-SA 3.0).

Page 74: *Taking a Sextant Reading Near the Beset* Terror. From *Narrative of an Expedition in HMS* Terror …, by George Back (London: John Murray, 1838). Courtesy of Toronto Public Library.

Page 75: Whetstone. Courtesy of Patricia Sutherland.

Page 76: *The Arctic Council planning a search for Sir John Franklin*, by Stephen Pearce (1851). © National Portrait Gallery, London.

Page 77: [Bottom] *Arctic Fox*. From *Narrative of a Second Voyage in Search of a North-West Passage …*, by John Ross (1835).

Page 78: [Top] *Enterprise* and *Investigator. The devils thumb, ships boring and warping in the pack*. Litho by Chas. Haghe after the original by Lieut. W. H. Browne; printed by Day & Son. Library of Congress, Prints & Photographs Division, LC-USZC4-11150. [Bottom] Panning for gold. Photo by L. C. McClure.

Page 79: David Woodman. Courtesy of David Woodman.

Page 80: Frederick Schwatka. Studio portrait by Bradley & Rulofson. Bibliothèque nationale de France / National Library of France.

Page 81: [Top] Map by Barb Kelly, based on map by David C. Woodman in "Inuit Tales of *Terror*: The location of Franklin's missing ship," 2016. [Bottom] Lieutenant Irving's grave. From *The Search for Franklin: A Narrative of the American Expedition under Lieutenant Schwatka, 1878 to 1880*. By Frederick Schwatka (London: T. Nelson and Sons, 1899).

Episode Six: No Retreat

Page 84: Sketch of *Terror*'s adapted steam locomotive engine from a letter Lieutenant John Irving sent his sister-in-law, Katie Irving, May 16, 1845. From *Sir John Franklin's Last Expedition to the Arctic Regions: A Memorial Sketch with Letters*, edited by Benjamin Bell (Edinburgh: David Douglas, 1881). University of Alberta Libraries, from original held by the Library of the Public Archives of Canada.

Page 85: *HMS* Erebus *in the ice, 1846*, by François Etienne Musin. National Maritime Museum, Greenwich, London, Caird Collection.

Page 86: Three modern icebreakers. Photo by Steve Wheeler/ USCG.

Page 87: [Top] *Crews of the* Isabella *and* Alexander *Sawing a Passage through the Ice*. From *A Voyage of Discovery, Made under the Orders of the Admiralty, in His Majesty's Ships* Isabella *and* Alexander …, by John Ross (London: John Murray, 1819). Courtesy of the John Carter Brown Library. [Bottom] Sir Ernest Shackleton's ship, *Endurance*. Library of Congress, Prints & Photographs Division, LC-USZ62-17176.

Page 88: Qilakitsoq mummies. Photo by David Stanley (CC BY 2.0).

Page 89: [Middle] Portrait of Jane Griffin. Lithograph by Joseph Mathias Negelen, after 1816 chalk drawing by Amelie Romilly. From *Portrait of Jane: A Life of Lady Franklin*, by Frances J. Woodward (London: Hodder and Stoughton, 1951). Library and Archives Canada/OCLC 2953470, 1951, frontispiece. [Bottom] Lady Franklin's flag. National Maritime Museum, Greenwich, London.

Page 90: "£20,000 Reward for the Discovery of the Missing Franklin Expedition," March 7, 1850. Library and Archives Canada / Library and Archives Canada Miscellaneous Poster Collection / e010754422.

Page 91: [Top] *Herald* and *Plover* in July 1849. From *Euryalus: Tales of the Sea, a Few Leaves from the Diary of a Midshipman*, by William Chimmo (1850). © British Library Board (10026.d.3).

Page 92: John Hartnell's Beechey Island grave marker. Alamy.

Page 93: [Top] Can of lead paint. Photo by Thester11 (CC BY 3.0). [Bottom] Dr. Jennie Christensen. Photo by Joyce McBeth.

Page 94: Exhuming John Hartnell's coffin. Photos by Brian Spenceley, courtesy of his family.

Page 95: [Top] John Hartnell's body. Photo by Brian Spenceley, courtesy of his family. [Bottom] Painting of an Inuit woman with tattoos on her face. Artist unknown (1654–). In *The Greenland Mummies*, by Jens Peder Hart Hansen, Jørgen Meldgaard, Jørgen Nordqvist (London: British Museum Publications, 1991).

Episode Seven: Landfall

Page 98: Watercolor of scurvy (1851). From the Historic Collections of the Institute of Naval Medicine, by kind permission of the Commanding Officer.

Page 99: *James Lind: Conqueror of Scurvy*, from "The History of Medicine," by Robert Thom. From the collection of Michigan Medicine, University of Michigan, Gift of Pfizer, Inc., UMHS.17.

Page 100: *The Albatross*. Engraving by Gustave Doré for an 1876 edition of the *Rime of the Ancient Mariner* by Samuel Coleridge.

Page 101: [Top] The *Erebus* and *Terror* in pack ice, in gale conditions, off the South Polar Ice Barrier, in the course of James. Clark Ross's 1839–1843 Antarctic expedition, January 1842. Chronicle/ Alamy Stock Photo.

Page 103: *Sir John Franklin's last moments*. Photograph of first work in a series of four frescoes by Julius V. Payer representing the final episode of John Franklin Expedition to the North Pole (1845), painted ca. 1883–1884 (Bruxelles, Belgium: ca.1932). Library and Archives Canada / Richard Julius Cyriax collection / PA-147988.

Page 104: *Captain William Penny*, by Stephen Pearce (1853). © National Portrait Gallery, London.

Page 105: [Top] *The Graves*. From the *Illustrated London News*, October 23, 1875. [Bottom] Ships *Lady Franklin, Sophia* and *Felix*. From *Journal of a Voyage in Baffin's Bay and Barrow Straits … Under the Command of Mr. William Penny …*, by Peter Sutherland (1852). Wellcome Collection. Public Domain Mark.

Page 106: [Top] Goldner-supplied canister. National Maritime Museum, Greenwich, London. [Bottom] Ridley's stripper harvester. State Library of South Australia B 8586.

Page 107: Arctic sea ice. Image courtesy of NASA's Scientific Visualization Studio, Goddard Space Flight Center.

Page 108: [Middle] Side-scan towfish. Jonathan Moore, Parks Canada. [Bottom] Part of a davit pintle and plan of *Erebus*. Jonathan Moore, Parks Canada.

Page 109: [Top] HMS *Erebus*, seen from above. Ryan Harris, Parks Canada. [Bottom] Ship's bell of the *Erebus*. Thierry Boyer, Parks Canada.

Episode Eight: Abandon Ship

Page 112: First Lieutenant Graham Gore. From the 1845 daguerreotype by Richard Beard.

Page 113: *A Funeral on the Ice. The Effect of Paraselenæ — Mock Moons*. From *The Voyage of the "Fox" in the Arctic Seas …*, by Francis Leopold McClintock (London: John Murray, 1859).

Page 114: [Top] Sir Francis Leopold McClintock, admiral, 1878, by Lock & Whitfield. Alamy. [Bottom] *Opening of the cairn on Point Victory, 1859*. From the *Illustrated London News*, October 15, 1859, page 366. Library and Archives Canada/OCLC 1752679.

Page 115: The 138-word Victory Point note. National Maritime Museum, Greenwich, London.

Page 116: *Noon in Mid-Winter.* From *Ten Coloured Views Taken during the Arctic Expedition of Her Majesty's Ships "Enterprise" and Investigator," under the Command of Captain Sir James C. Ross.* Print by William Henry Browne. (London: Ackerman & Co., 1850). © British Library Board 1259.d.11.

Page 117: Adapted from detail of *Map of the North West Part of Canada, Hudson's Bay & Indian Territories,* Drawn by Thos. Devine by Order of the Honble Joseph Cauchon, Comm of Crown Lands. Toronto, March 1857. Original and digitized map are in McMaster University's Lloyd Reeds Map Collection.

Page 118: Relics of the Franklin expedition. From the *Illustrated London News,* October 15, 1859. Image from *The Franklin Mystery: Life and Death in the Arctic* (www.canadianmysteries.ca).

Page 119: [Top] *Abandoning the Vessels.* Photograph of second work in a series of four frescoes by Julius V. Payer representing the final episode of John Franklin Expedition to the North Pole (1845), painted ca. 1883–1884. (Bruxelles, Belgium: ca. 1932). Library and Archives Canada / Richard Julius Cyriax collection / e011184624.

Page 120: Inside a meat-preserving factory. *Illustrated London News,* January 31, 1852, page 93.

Page 121: Sledge parties. From *The Eventful Voyage of H.M. Discovery Ship* Resolute *to the Arctic Regions in Search of Sir John Franklin …,* by George F. McDougall (London: Longman, Brown, Green, Longmans, & Roberts, 1857).

Page 122: [Top] Goldner-supplied cans left behind. National Maritime Museum, Greenwich, London.

Page 123: A "bone detective" examines deer bones. Jackie Ricciardi, *The Brink.*

Page 124: [Top] English Harbour. Roy Johnson, dbimages / Alamy Stock Photo.

Episode Nine: The Unthinkable

Page 128: Lieutenant Henry LeVesconte. From the 1845 daguerreotype by Richard Beard.

Page 129: *The Crew of HMS* Terror *Saving the Boats and Provisions on the Night of 15th March (1837),* 1838, by George Hyde Chambers. Collection of the Beaverbrook Art Gallery, 1981.04.

Page 130: *Division of Sledges Passing Cape Lady Franklin; Extraordinary Masses of Ice Pressed Against the North Shore of Bathurst Island,* 1855. W5516 © New Brunswick Museum – Musée du Nouveau-Brunswick.

Page 132: [Top] *Sir John Franklin's Men Dying by Their Boat During the North-West Passage Expedition,* by W. Thomas Smith. National Maritime Museum, Greenwich, London. [Bottom] A mummy from Zeleny Yar. Yamalo-Nenets Regional Museum and Exhibition Complex.

Page 133: [Left] Portrait of John Rae, by William Armstrong. Glenbow Museum, Calgary. [Right] Map of John Rae's travels. Display panel at Stromness Museum, Orkney.

Page 135: [Top] "The Lost Arctic Voyages," from *Household Words, A Weekly Journal Conducted by Charles Dickens.* Saturday, December 23, 1854. [Bottom] Map from *On the Mode of Communication of Cholera,* by John Snow (London: C.F. Cheffins, 1854).

Page 136: [Left] Sketch map of King William Land provided by In-nook-poo-zhee-jook to Charles Francis Hall, 1869. From *Narrative of the Second Arctic Expedition Made by Charles F. Hall …* Original image from the Biodiversity Heritage Library.

Page 137: [Middle] Sammy Kogvik. Arctic Research Foundation. [Bottom] Adrian Schimnowski. Meaghan Brackenbury / Cabin Radio.

Page 138: Side-scan sonar image of HMS *Terror.* Ryan Harris, Parks Canada.

Page 139: HMS *Terror's* wheel. Thierry Boyer, Parks Canada.

Episode Ten: Last Days

Page 142: *Sledging over Hummocky Ice.* From *A Series of Eight Sketches in Colour (Together with a Chart of the Route) by Lieut. S. Gurney Cresswell, of the Voyage of H.M.S.* Investigator *(Captain M'Clure), during the Discovery of the North-West Passage.* University of Calgary Archives and Special Collections, Arctic Institute of North America Collection.

Page 143: [Top] *Manellia and Adelik,* an Inuit family. From *Narrative of a Second Voyage in Search of a North-West Passage …,* by John Ross (1835). Image from the Biodiversity Heritage Library. [Bottom] Fort Resolution. Artokoloro / Alamy.

Page 144: Inuit girls and women. Portrait by Edward Augustus Inglefield; National Maritime Museum, Greenwich, London.

Page 145: Detail from *Map of the North West Part of Canada, Hudson's Bay & Indian Territories,* Drawn by Thos. Devine by Order of the Honble Joseph Cauchon, Comm of Crown Lands. Toronto, March 1857. Original and digitized map are in the McMaster University Lloyd Reeds Map Collection.

Page 146: Pocket chronometer from HMS *Terror.* National Maritime Museum, Greenwich, London.

Page 147: [Middle] Captain Sir Leopold McClintock, R. N., L.L.D, 1860. Library and Archives Canada / National Archives of Canada Print collection / e010955935. [Bottom] *The Fox on a Rock Near Buchan Island.* From *The Voyage of the "Fox" in the Arctic Seas…,* by Francis Leopold McClintock. © British Library Board (10460.d.2).

Page 148: [Top] *Captain McClintock's First Interview with the Esquimaux at Cape Victoria.* From the *Illustrated London News,* October 8, 1859, p. 355. [Bottom] *Discovery of the Franklin Expedition Boat on King William's Land by Lieutenant Hobson.* An illustration from an original wood engraving from the collection of Russell A. Potter. *Harper's Weekly* 1859, Vol. 3, pages 696–697.

Page 149: Map drawn by Oonalee, Netsilingmiut man, in 1859 showing the location where he told Captain F. L. McClintock that one of Franklin's ships had sunk off Kiikertaksuak (King William Island) (1859). Royal Geographical Society, London, Francis Leopold McClintock Collection, Reference No. SSC-105-3. / *The Franklin Mystery: Life and Death in the Arctic* (www.canadianmysteries.ca).

Page 150: [Top] The Sir John Franklin Expedition Memorial, Royal Naval College in Greenwich. Courtesy of Jacqueline Banerjee, Victorian Web Foundation. [Bottom] The only known photo of Lady Franklin and Sophy Cracroft. Detail of a stereograph. Courtesy of the George Eastman Museum.

Page 153: [Top] Officers of the Franklin Expedition, photographs from a mounted set of daguerreotype portraits made by Richard Beard in May 1845 (D8760/F/LIB/8/1/5). Courtesy of Derbyshire Record Office. [Bottom] Douglas Stenton at NgLj-3 on King William Island. Photo by Robert W. Park, courtesy of Douglas Stenton.

Page 154: [Top] *Man Proposes, God Disposes,* by Sir Edwin Landseer. By permission of Royal Holloway, University of London. [Bottom] Captain Francis Crozier. From the 1845 daguerreotype by Richard Beard.

Page 155: A drone's view of support barge above wreck of *Erebus.* Thierry Boyer, Parks Canada.

Page 159: Cornelius Hickey's knife. National Maritime Museum, Greenwich, London, Greenwich Hospital Collection.

To all the members of the Explorers Club
and all your amazing adventures – S.B.

Published in Canada and the U.S. by Kids Can Press Ltd.
25 Dockside Drive, Toronto, ON M5A 0B5

Kids Can Press is a Corus Entertainment Inc. company
www.kidscanpress.com

The text is set in Myriad Pro and Stone Informal.

Edited by Kathleen Fraser
Designed by Barb Kelly

Printed and bound in Shenzhen, China,
in 10/2021 by C & C Offset

CM 22 0 9 8 7 6 5 4 3 2 1

Library and Archives Canada Cataloguing in Publication

Title: Trapped in Terror Bay : solving the mystery of the lost Franklin Expedition / Sigmund Brouwer.
Other titles: Solving the mystery of the lost Franklin Expedition
Names: Brouwer, Sigmund, 1959– author.
Identifiers: Canadiana 20200401483 | ISBN 9781525303456 (hardcover)
Subjects: LCSH: Franklin, John, 1786-1847—Juvenile literature. | LCSH: Crozier, Francis Rawdon Moira, 1796-1848 — Juvenile literature. | LCSH: John Franklin Arctic Expedition (1845-1851) — Juvenile literature. | LCSH: Terror (Ship) — Juvenile literature. | LCSH: Erebus (Ship) — Juvenile literature. | LCSH: Canada, Northern — Discovery and exploration British — Juvenile literature. | LCSH: Northwest Passage — Discovery and exploration — British Juvenile literature.
Classification: LCC FC3961.3 .B76 2021 | DDC j917.1904/1 — dc23

Kids Can Press gratefully acknowledges that the land on which our office is located is the traditional territory of many nations, including the Mississaugas of the Credit, the Anishnabeg, the Chippewa, the Haudenosaunee and the Wendat peoples, and is now home to many diverse First Nations, Inuit and Métis peoples.

We thank the Government of Ontario, through Ontario Creates; the Ontario Arts Council; the Canada Council for the Arts; and the Government of Canada for supporting our publishing activity.